Praise for *The Chromebook Infused Classroom*

"This is *the* book for teachers using Chromebooks in the classrooms. Read it, highlight it, and share it with other educators so all teachers can learn how to take their already great analog lessons and create powerful digital learning experiences. *The Chromebook Infused Classroom* is a happy combination of sound pedagogy and powerful classroom tech that we all need as we move forward into a new normal for teaching."

—**Matt Miller**, speaker, blogger, and author of *Tech Like a Pirate* and *Ditch That Textbook*

"Has your school deployed Chromebooks and now you're wondering how to teach with them? *The Chromebook Infused Classroom* is a must-have resource for all classroom teachers ready to take digital learning to the next level. The Chromebook is just the vehicle for learning. Holly Clark walks you through how to drive this vehicle for powerful instructional opportunities and authentic learning for your students. This is a book you need on your desk to refer back to often as a road map to elevate your blended learning experiences from assigning to instruction."

—**Lisa Highfill**, coauthor of *The HyperDoc Handbook*

"This book is a must-read for all educators. Like the other Infused Classroom books, *The Chromebook Infused Classroom* puts pedagogy at the center of learning and helps teachers see how they can take their great analog work and make it powerfully digital. This book lifts up student voice, which results in better learning opportunities for all students."

—**Jornea Armant**, @Savvy_Educator, education innovation lead at Flipgrid

"*The Chromebook Infused Classroom* provides a fantastic combination of big ideas and actionable information. You'll find the best practices to lay a foundation for strong teaching and learning with technology alongside activities you can use tomorrow to help students interact and create in digital spaces. If you're teaching in a Chromebook classroom, add this book to your reading list!"

—**Monica Burns**, EdD, founder of ClassTechTips.com and author of *Tasks Before Apps*

"A Chromebook is *not* just a digital textbook meant to be passively read and used for multiple-choice quizzes. To be effective, technology such as Chromebooks should be used in ways that engage students and help them create and personalize their learning for a Goldilocks experience that is 'just right.' Research has shown that adding a device to a classroom without a pedagogical shift is actually *subtractive* academically. Thank the moon for Holly Clark and this book. With her clear, concise, and inspired lesson planning along with 'just right' examples, Clark makes teaching with a Chromebook easier and more effective."

—**Jon Corippo**, speaker, teacher, and coauthor of *The EduProtocol Fieldguide*

Holly Clark

THE
CHROMEBOOK
INFUSED
CLASSROOM

USING BLENDED LEARNING to CREATE
ENGAGING, STUDENT-CENTERED CLASSROOMS

Foreword by Kasey Bell

Edited by Maryann Rose

The Chromebook Infused Classroom
©2020 by Holly Clark

These books are available at special discounts when purchased in quantity for use as premiums, promotions, fundraising and educational use. For inquiries and details, contact the publisher: info@elevatebooksedu.com.

Published by ElevateBooksEdu

Library of Congress Control Number: On File
Paperback ISBN: 978-1-7334814-9-6
ebook ISBN: 978-1-7352046-0-4

Some artwork designed by Monica Isabel Martinez @mpowerdesigns
basic graphics from vecteezy.com

BRING MEANINGFUL AND HIGH-ENERGY PD
TO YOUR SCHOOL OR EVENT

The Chromebook Infused Classroom Learning Workshops are firmly grounded in research-based pedagogy. These professional development (PD) sessions show teachers how to create powerful blended learning lessons to support our modern learners as the classroom environment shifts from analog to digital.

The COVID-19 Virus made it necessary for us all to understand the importance of digital pedagogies. Now it's time to take what we established during this period of distance learning and build on it so we can make learning more meaningful, whether teaching is remote or face-to-face.

Chromebook Infused professional learning engagements help teachers learn to:

⤷ Craft student-facing blended lessons

⤷ Create more meaningful digital assessments

⤷ Understand how to use digital learning tools for richer differentiation

⤷ Create demonstrations of learning that allow students to apply and transfer knowledge

Chromebook Infused PD supports those who might not have been inclined to learn and teach with new digital pedagogies and tools. Teachers already familiar with it will enjoy learning the research-based pedagogy to help them take their practice even further.

Together, teachers will learn to create engaging, student-centered learning that supports the modern skills our students and teachers must develop in a changing world.

To inquire about online sessions and professional learning days, or to schedule Holly as a speaker, fill out the form at **infused.link/pd**.

For an example, see **infused.link/pdexample** (this is one with an iPad and Chromebook school).

CONTENTS

1 ▸ A LITTLE BACKGROUND...

17 ▸ A QUICK LOOK ... TIME TO GET IN THE KNOW

39 ▸ THE CHROMEBOOK INFUSED CLASSROOM

61 ▸ THE CHROMEBOOK INFUSED STUDENT

FOREWORD

I've always been what people call an early adopter—willing to try new technology and test it out in my classroom—even when it means falling flat on my face. Then came Google and what eventually became known as Google for Education, and that changed everything. Because I'm the crazy teacher who is always trying new technology, I was actually using Google Docs before it was owned by Google, back when it was this little app called Writely. Before I graduated with my master's in edtech, Google had acquired Writely, changed the name, and changed word processing forever.

Fast forward to 2011, before I was a blogger. I had heard tales of these new devices coming from Google, more netbook than laptop—if anyone reading this is old enough to remember netbooks. At the time, I was working at a regional service center in Texas and delivering training to schools in the Dallas region. The number one topic at the time was the iPad. Schools were scrambling to invest in these touch-screen dazzlers. But iPads were expensive, a nightmare to manage at schools, and a bit of a stretch to get into the hands of all students.

The Chromebook swooped in at a much lower price point, running a light OS, and gradually changing the landscape of school-owned devices forever. The Chromebook offered many things that the iPad and even more robust laptops failed to deliver. It is an affordable device, easy to use, easy to update, and, more importantly, it ushered in the age of one-to-one schools. Educational technology, and my career, was changed forever.

As I have said for many years, Google plays well with others, which is something Apple products, and others have not done. So the Chromebook allowed teachers and students to use hundreds of web-based tools, most without heavy and timely installations and shared across users. The conversation quickly shifted from which schools I worked with that had tried this new Google thing, to what schools were still resisting "Going Google."

Now, we are many years into the evolution of the Chromebook of Google for Education as a service, and schools have access to more devices than ever before. Don't get me wrong; the technology is only as good as its facilitator. I've seen teachers innovate their classrooms with only a few devices, but I've also seen one-to-one classes use Chromebooks as nothing more than an overpriced workbook or textbook. That's where *The Chromebook Infused Classroom* comes in!

Holly Clark and I have been friends for several years now, and we both believe in the importance of good pedagogy, doing new things with digital tools, and that technology can revolutionize education. When I wrote my first book, *Shake Up Learning: Practical Ideas to Move Learning From Static to Dynamic*, I asked Holly to write an endorsement. As she read her early access copy, she texted me every few pages with a high five and revealed how our pedagogical thinking is so aligned.

Knowing and understanding Holly's Infused Classroom Framework, and combining that with the power of a Chromebook and Google tools will change your mindset. What you learn here will increase your confidence and shake up your classroom in ways you never thought possible.

Are you ready to change the game? This is it, y'all! Take it away, Holly!

—Kasey Bell
Google Certified Innovator and Trainer,
and Infused Classroom fangirl!

JOIN THE COMMUNITY

 @HollyClarkEdu

 @HollyClarkEdu

 HollyClark.org

 EdSpace.live

 facebook.com/groups/
infusedclassroom

pinterest.com/
theinfusedclassroom

INTRODUCTION

Why the Infused Classroom?
Why Did I Write This Book?

Take a journey with me back in time for a moment to Holly Clark circa 1996, in San Francisco, California. If you need a song choice to take you back to 1996, think "The Macarena" or Tupac's "California Love."

I was a student teacher, and I remember watching *The Dead Poets Society*, thinking to myself, I want to be *THAT* teacher: the one who thinks differently, does things differently, and inspires students to fall in love with learning. I wanted to be the teacher who brought meaning and excitement into the classroom. I thought to myself, I want to be so good someday that students would stand on desks in an "O Captain, My Captain" moment that would somehow justify my creative take on education.

I started teaching in San Francisco at the exact moment that high-speed internet was coming to big cities. Early adopters were starting to witness the power of this shift in information, and hearts pumped faster as we realized what this meant. As I became familiar with what this new superhighway of information could do, I knew I had found that "O Captain, My Captain" moment! I knew instinctively that technology would enable me to become that educator of my student teacher dreams. So I hurried off to graduate school at Teachers College, Columbia University, and returned to a new teaching assignment in a Silicon Valley classroom, ready to change the world.

One back-to-school night, I confessed my crazy idea to parents—that computers would open a new world of learning for students, and I couldn't wait until the day we all had computers in our classrooms. For now, though, I had built a website for homework and resources and would be taking students to the school's computer lab as often as I possibly could. After my talk, one of the parents tapped me on the shoulder. "Ms. Clark, I would like to introduce myself. I own one of the big tech firms here in town, and I want to give you a computer *for every student* and see what you can do with them."

That was September 2000.

The next day, twenty-five eMachines arrived. I opened the door to accept them and turned around to all the startled looks on my students' faces as I reveled in my Oprah

Winfrey moment: *You* get a computer! And *you* get a computer! And *you* get a computer! In unison, they all squealed and jumped up and down as if I were handing out cars. In their minds, they had won the seventh-grade lottery. Instinctively, I knew their excitement came from the realization that this moment was a turning point. Learning was about to change in our classroom.

As I turned around from the excitement to speak to the men delivering the devices, one of them handed me a note with one simple request:

"Dear Ms. Clark:

Here is my contribution. Show the world what technology can do for education."

It was no longer about me and my "O Captain, My Captain" moment. It couldn't be about me. At that time, I had no blogs to follow, no books to read on the subject, no social media from which to gather ideas. Even more, I could not do this alone. I had to change my mindset and let the students become my partners in learning. I had to learn to both trust and guide.

Imagine what I saw as we began to make use of the devices and shifted to a student-centered classroom. Instead of sitting at desks like compliant learners, my students were investigating, challenging, and learning how to form their own opinions. Instead of waiting for answers from their teacher, these kids were empowered to ask thought-provoking questions, and technology meant they had the means to find the answers for themselves. Instead of ME being in charge of the learning, THEY learned to think, to question and to create powerful learning experiences—for themselves.

What happened that year transformed my ideas about teaching and learning. While taking copious notes, I reflected on the changes I witnessed. I delved deeply into research about the way people learn so I could make sure the changes we were making benefitted my students. As I critically watched, students made connections that led them to deep and effective learning. At a time when the world was fascinated with *Bridget Jones's Diary*, I was taking a deep dive into the discoveries my students were making and writing a diary of my own—about how technology was affecting the academic growth of my students. The results were astonishing.

Parents also cheered me on as I tried new strategies. Instead of complaining their kids were getting too much screen time or protesting that grades were online, they were asking questions and taking their own notes. We took a novel approach to our learning, putting aside textbooks and collaborating in groups via Blackboard Chat Rooms after school. No one objected or complained. I truly believe today that effective technology, engaged students, supportive parents, and our school's location in Silicon Valley—the cradle of the tech industry—created the perfect storm of change, and it was fast and furious!

Every day, my students ran to class, were more engaged in learning, and began to think deeply and grapple with ideas and content. Test scores rose, and soon I was getting the results that made administrators start to ask questions about what was happening in my classroom. It was exhilarating!

Cut to today in 2020.

Since that time, I have brought that same academic success to many schools, both public and private, in rural areas and the inner city as a teacher. As a coach, I have logged nearly one million air miles visiting schools around the world, helping teachers make the kind of changes that worked in my classroom. Through the Infused Classroom, I work to help teachers rethink what powerful teaching and learning can look like in the twenty-first century. I have spent time studying at Harvard, digging into research, wrestling through opposing views and weighing those against the results I have seen. In addition, I stand firm today in my belief that if done right, we can help students become deep thinkers with an insatiable love for learning—while achieving top scores on achievement tests. It comes from putting pedagogy and cognitive learning strategies first and using the learning tool of technology to empower learning in classrooms.

This does not happen overnight; it takes a reimagining of nearly everything we learned in teacher training and experienced ourselves as students.

I have collected all of these ideas into this book because I want teachers who have been given Chromebooks to not have to do all the work I did. Most people don't have time to study the way I did, to visit schools the way I do, and to critically analyze every teaching strategy they use.

What follows on the pages of this book are ideas based on twenty-plus years of teaching in a variety of circumstances. I invite you to comb through the ideas in this book and take what works for you—implement only those practices that resonate with you. **I ask one favor, however. Just like the generous parent who wanted me to "show the world what technology can do for education," I ask that you do the same.** Use the tools that will prepare your students to tackle the world's greatest challenges—and be "Captains" of their own futures.

Together let's show the world what technology can do for education!

—Holly
#infusedclassroom
hollyclark.org

HOW TO USE THIS BOOK

Although this book is based on careful research, data gathering, and experience, it is not new pedagogy. It is a practical, hands-on guide for using technology to support the already solid pedagogy happening in classrooms around the globe. Feel free to skim through for ideas that resonate with you—don't worry about what you can't use in your classroom and make a mess on these pages! Highlight, doodle, color-code, and bookmark to enrich teaching and learning in your classroom.

QR Code Directions You will see many QR codes scattered throughout the book. This is where the author will come to life to explain a concept in more depth or to give you a quick tip.

To watch the videos, download the Flipgrid app on your mobile device.

Open app and select Scan Flipgrid QR and point at QR code.

Then 'Holly' will pop up and explain something in Augmented Reality (AR). It will be a fun way to interact with the book!

Reflection

It's important to keep a running log of practices and tools you used in the classroom:

- What activated curiosity?
- What made students feel successful?
- Where did you see students take charge of their learning?
- How is this affecting the learning environment?
- Did anything work better than you predicted?
- Did anything fall short of your expectations?

INTERACT WITH THE BOOK IN THE WAY THAT WORKS BEST FOR YOU!

Analog

When you find an idea or tool that inspires you, use tools like these to mark your place, write your reflections, and ask questions:

- Highlighters
- Colored Pens
- Sticky notes
- Stickers
- Bookmarks

Digital

Don't forget to keep a Google Doc or use an online storage tool to be able to refer back to online resources:

- Keep a Wakelet Collection of useful links you find in this book, use something like Google Drive or Google Keep, or even a folder on your computer desktop.

- Add links to resources and websites you find on your own.

On the next page of the book, you will find links to join the online community and get into the conversation with Infused Classroom colleagues.

Join the Infused Classroom Facebook Group to learn about free book study groups.

facebook.com/groups/infusedclassroom

Share the light-bulb moments you saw in the classroom. Offer suggestions and ask questions of your own. Infused Classroom teachers and learners are always evolving and growing together!

A LITTLE BACKGROUND...

Flipgrid AR

Holly Clark

Why Chromebooks?

If you are reading this book because your school admin just bought Chromebooks, rest assured they made a pretty amazing decision. Compared to standard laptop computers, Chromebooks are easier to manage in a classroom and more durable with longer battery life. These devices are a well-constructed, cost-effective way for educators to bridge the gap between students who have access to technology and those who don't. Chromebooks contribute to creating equity and democratizing education. Teachers and students who carry them in hand should be proud to be part of a revolution that IS going to change the way schools provide comprehensive and effective education.

Chromebooks have taken the education world by storm, in part because of the simpler operating system. Google Drive, although cloud-based, can be used offline so that students who might not have internet access at home do not need to fall behind their peers. In addition, if you are worried about the littles (younger grades like K–2), there is a touch screen version that works similarly to an iPad—but is more cost-effective—that helps the younger student develop important motor skills. Chromebooks are an incredibly versatile addition to any classroom. They:

⇨ Give students access to information.

⇨ Provide authentic collaboration opportunities.

- Connect students beyond the four walls of the classroom with students from other classrooms and experts in a variety of subjects.

- Develop skills students will need for future job success in a rapidly changing world.

- Assist teachers in applying the inquiry process and allowing students to ask more meaningful questions.

- Promote a global perspective and cultivate empathy.

- Amplify teaching and learning in the classroom.

The Chromebook is built for the twenty-first century, so trying to use it for twentieth-century teaching methods won't work as well. The educator who implements the ideas in this book must understand the need for a seismic shift in pedagogical practice and embrace that shift.

If you are a classroom teacher, effectively using Chromebooks in your curriculum might be a new and scary experience. Maybe you are familiar with Chromebooks, but you need additional ideas and support. Most educators learned their craft in the twentieth century without constant and real-time access to information, so adapting your teaching to the infusion of technology in this new way can be intimidating. Have no fear! We hope to get you on the path to teaching and learning with these versatile devices. By applying what you learn from this book, you will grow more comfortable using them in your daily practice.

Together, we will revolutionize your instruction step-by-step and successfully infuse Chromebooks into your classrooms. You are well on your way, and this book will help!

> If you want to take a deep dive into the strategies in this book from the author and a host of experts—you can join The Chromebook Infused Classroom Online Course. (Use code: BOOK). Go to **infused.link/online** to learn more.

UNDERSTANDING OUR
GENERATION Z LEARNERS

Now that you understand the power of having Chromebooks, it is time to understand why technology is so important for our students.

Today's students are *not* different learners, but they do live in a world where *how* we learn is making a dramatic shift. In most cases, teacher credentialing programs have not kept up with this shift, and now teachers are coming to work unprepared for this new landscape of information and learning. This is not the fault of any one person, but it does require that teachers continue to learn in order to meet the needs of our Generation Z students.

Our Generation Z Learners

The Student Voice Infused Classroom   @HollyClarkEdu

First students to be born into a world with smartphones, tablets and computers.

They like information in bite-sized chunks and prefer hands-on learning.

They talk in images and emojis, and they prefer YouTube to TV.

For Gen Z it's easier to gain an audience, a stage, and the attention of the right people, i.e. Parkland Students

Their social circle is global.

They are social entrepreneurs and like their learning to have meaning and purpose.

Don't stand for the status quo.

Born into an information revolution i.e. from artificial intelligence, self-driving cars and drones, to virtual assistants

They like to make and create.

They want to connect, collaborate and share.

@rbathursthunt   HollyClark.org

Who are these students?

Generation Z kids were born after 1995, which means almost every kid sitting in our classrooms is from this generation. They are NOT millennials. If you have younger kids, they are Generation Alpha and we still know little about them.

Gen Z students are the first kids born into a technology-rich world, and technology is invisible to them. They easily handle smartphones, tablets, and computers.

They are the first students to be born AG—After Google. In fact, Gen Z kids don't know a world without Google. It is an integral part of their daily lives, but in some cases NOT at the institutions of learning they attend. (Enter Chromebooks!)

They are hyper-connected, but as the authors of *The Gen Z Effect* Tom Koulopoulos and Dan Keldsen claim, "They are not as much tech savvy as they are tech-dependent." Their phones are the hub of their social lives, but they don't do phone calls. They do texts—well, not really texts—they communicate with acronyms and images like GIFs, Emojis, and TikToks.

Claire Madden, Australia's foremost social researcher on generational engagement, notes in her book *Hello Gen Z*, "They are the largest, most technologically savvy, socially networked and globally connected generation in history."

Like the generations before them, Gen Z learners enjoy hands-on learning. They really want to be able to connect, collaborate, and share.

Their familiarity with technology and social media makes them born social entrepreneurs.

They are passionate—they want to change the world! So many of them are doing just that, but sadly it's happening outside the classroom.

They are learning right in the middle of an information revolution, which is exciting because they have access to information never before seen in human history. But it's also terrifying because we don't know how this enormous shift will affect our classrooms and curriculum.

Gen Z learners are the first ones to tell you that their attention spans are short, that they feel constantly wired, and that they need multiple senses stimulated to be able to engage and learn.

For fun, take a look at this video about our Gen Z students. The video (bit.ly/infusedgenz) humorously claims that this generation has an eight-second attention span. They think in small, bite-sized chunks of information, and they get most of their information from Google. For this reason, they also need to evaluate information, learn about bias, and become expert fact-checkers. We have to teach them the value of deep work and deep learning.

Claire Madden, author of *Hello Gen Z*, also says that for this generation, technology has done the following:

- Sharpened their thinking
- Facilitated communication
- Redefined community
- Become core to their learning

But these kids can utilize even short attention spans if we help them. They can grow to be creators and amazing problem-solvers. They are keenly aware that the world is leaving them with some big problems that they will need to solve. We need to equip them with this problem-solving skill.

Story From The Field

When a problem faces this generation of students, they use their voices to challenge the status quo. For example, inspiring students from Marjory Stoneman Douglas High School in Parkland, Florida, followed in the footsteps of their namesake, the women's suffrage activist, to protest gun violence. Taking to social media, they organized a March on Washington, D.C. and high schools around the nation. Their immediate and well-executed actions told the world that they are the generation who refuses to sit by and accept problems the adults cannot fix. They believe they can create change, and they use technology to further their cause. They are the poster children for student agency and what *this* generation can and will accomplish! And we get to teach these amazing kids! Lucky us!

Enter Teacher-preneurs.

In this information revolution, we can become teacher-preneurs, creating classrooms we only dreamt about as kids—the kind of classrooms that enable kids to activate curiosity, develop multiple skills, explore for themselves, and fall in love with problem-solving. Our classrooms don't have to be incubators of memorization and multiple-choice tests. We must build new classrooms where curiosity is center-stage.

The fact is that Generation Z is growing up at the forefront of an amazing information revolution. They see technology not as an add-on, but central to their lives. As their teachers, we should view it the same way. This generation has access to the information and familiarity with tech devices, so let them use those things to become inquirers and problem-solvers. They need to develop the curiosity, empathy, and compassion that will change the world. One day, a student in one of your classes might just be the person who comes up with the cure for cancer. That will never happen, though, if we do not equip them with skills to ask big questions and solve even bigger problems.

Special Note: Although they are still quite young, the next generation—children born after 2010—is referred to as Gen Alpha. They are still becoming their own force, but they will come out of school at the end of the 2030s. This is the decade that will see the largest influx of information we have ever seen, when artificial intelligence will be a powerful force. Because of this, educators have to rethink what is important. Is it only facts regurgitated on a test? Or is it using information to find your passion and develop a love of learning that will foster future success? Our job is shifting. The classroom is shifting. Now it's time to think of yourself not as simply an instructor, but as the guide on the ride!

Understanding CHROMEBOOKS and Digital Pedagogies

ARE WE READY FOR 5G AND AI?

The Seismic Shift in Information That Will Impact Your Classroom

You understand the *why* of Chromebooks, a little bit more about your *Gen Z learners*, and now it's time for some real talk.

Prepare yourself. Fifth-generation wireless, or 5G, designed to revolutionize wireless networks by supercharging their speed and responsiveness, is becoming mainstream in many countries.

This significant jump in speed will have an unprecedented impact on all kinds of professions with the proliferation of **artificial intelligence (AI)** technology, or the ability of technology to simulate human intelligence. AI processes include learning, reasoning, and self-correction. It will soon be a major component of our society, impacting daily life and **creating a distinctly different job market—one that awaits our students when they graduate.**

Understanding Artificial Intelligence

The implementation of 5G means that AI will function at supercharged speeds. Tech pioneer and author of the groundbreaking book *AI Superpowers*, Kai-Fu Lee, spoke to reporter Scott Pelley on CBS's *60 Minutes* and made this bold claim: **"I believe [AI] is going to change the world more than anything in the history of mankind—more than electricity.** The difference between the robot revolution and other revolutions that have disrupted the labor markets is the **rate of change."** Along with that, Lee stated, "The inventions of the steam engine, the sewing machine, [and] electricity have all displaced jobs. And we've gotten over it. The challenge of AI is this: AI will increasingly replace repetitive jobs, not just for blue-collar work, but a lot of white-collar work. Chauffeurs, truck drivers, anyone who does driving for a living—their jobs will be disrupted more in the next fifteen to twenty-five year time frame." He continued, "Many jobs that seem a little bit complex, [like a] chef [or] waiter, ... will become automated. In fifteen years, [AI will] displace about forty percent of the jobs in the world."

How Do We Prepare Students?

How do we prepare students for a world in which our job markets will change dramatically? The answers are multi-faceted and unknown. We can guess, and here are two:

First, it means your Alexa, Google Home, or Apple Watch are about to get their own version of a flux capacitor. (It's hard not to use a *Back to the Future* reference in times like these. Which means we must focus less on facts.)

Second, it means that AI will begin to function at unimaginable levels. On his podcast *Exponential Wisdom*, Peter Diamandis claims that this change will be so massive in scale that we haven't even seen one percent of the change we are going to see in the next decade. We have to help students be able to quickly pivot in their jobs as global unknowns often disrupt normal routines.

Based on these two examples, we have to ask ourselves three questions:

1. Does this mean we are living in a modern-day dark age right now?

2. How will this seismic shift in information technology impact our classrooms and learning standards?

3. What effect will this shift in information have on the way we learn?

Without knowing the answers to these questions, we know that AI is already functioning in our daily lives. From Google and Apple Maps GPS to Alexa, Google Home, and Siri, AI is an integral part of many of our life experiences and daily routines. It is also becoming a distinct revolutionary force in many industries because a defining aspect of AI is deep learning. AI provides an avenue to make deeper and more important connections. Think of consumer services like AncestryDNA or 23andMe. Thanks to AI, these companies can now tell you your health risks and propensities with startling accuracy (It even tells you if you like cilantro!). You can find your long-lost relatives and even predict what your descendants will look like based on your genome as far ahead as fifty years. Law enforcement now utilizes these two platforms to solve decades-old cold-case crimes.

5G and the Changing Labor Landscape

Tech experts predict that many of the common labor jobs such as drivers—truck, ambulance, bus, and Uber drivers—will be disrupted in the next ten to fifteen years as self-driving cars become more prevalent. Some reports claim that driving is one of the most populated industries, so automation will have a huge impact on employment if people are not able to adjust to a changing market. Retail sales floor jobs, the most populated job as of 2019, will also go through dramatic shifts as more computer-based ordering and checkout systems that are powered by AI replace cashiers. Those AI checkouts we see in many McDonald's and supermarkets will soon be present everywhere.

We also know that *where* people do their jobs is also being disrupted. Some statistics indicate the number of telecommuters is at 50 percent of the workforce and growing each year. After COVID-19 this is sure to grow exponentially. With this shift, additional skills will be needed to work from home, like a strict focus on project and time management skills and financial literacies. As of yet, these skills are not often taught in schools.

The Arrival of AI Forces Us as Educators to Ask Three Questions:

1. What effect will this increase in the speed of information have on the way we learn?

2. How will this seismic shift in information technology impact our classrooms and learning standards?

3. With this inevitable progression, can we afford to resist this change and drag our feet in the integration of technology in all of our classrooms?

Educators don't need to fear AI—it will supercharge the use of data to more quickly solve complex issues. In the future, it may well help to find solutions to humanity's greatest problems, like the global climate crisis or a cure for cancer. It has endless possibilities for improving human lives, but we must be prepared for it. In our classrooms, it will mean we are not so locked into teaching facts but beginning to shift toward inquiry and deeper learning.

Technology is disrupting not only the work environment but the educational environment as well. Faster information and the ability to quickly download graphics have allowed some schools to use virtual reality (VR) in ways unimaginable even a few years ago. Take, for example, a high school biology class at The American School of Madrid. This student goes virtually inside a nucleosome to identify its components using VR. Watch the experience here:

🖎 Check out this video on **infused.link/example**

This example is Before 5G

Source: David Hotler (@dhotler) of The American School of Madrid

Adaptable and flexible educators are using technology and social platforms to engage in meaningful conversations and form professional learning networks. They glean important information that was not available even two decades ago. **In a 5G learning environment, multiple-choice tests and the decades-old syllabus are left in the dust!**

The bottom line is that if we are going to get ready for 5G learning and 5G-equipped students, using our Chromebooks for authentic, problem-based learning experiences will be indispensable. We don't have a choice. We don't have time to debate the usefulness of Chromebooks in the classroom, but we need to find the time to learn how to use them for more powerful learning—and quickly!

The Future of Chromebooks with Augmented and Virtual Reality

Special Spotlight: Jesse Lubinsky Co-author of *Reality Bytes: Innovative Learning Using Augmented and Virtual Reality* Infused.link/realitybytes

While artificial intelligence is helping to push the boundaries of what is possible through use of a Chromebook, it isn't the only emergent technology creating new visions of what is possible for our students.

AR is when technology is used to superimpose information on top of the world we see. The information can range from simple text to more detailed images, audio, and video. One great application for leveraging the power of AR using Chromebooks is Metaverse. Metaverse allows both teachers and students to create AR experiences in their classrooms on their Chromebooks. Students can create engaging interactive stories and "scavenger hunts" that allow them to share their creativity and learning with their peers.

Unlike AR, which blends digital objects with the real world, VR takes things to the next level with completely simulated digital environments. VR takes almost any type of content and creates **immersive experiences** to enhance teaching and learning. You can easily build VR spaces using your Chromebook with CoSpaces EDU. Students can use VR to model ideas in science, literature, or history.

For more information, check out our work around AR and VR at Ready Learner One (**readylearner.one**)

SHIFTING FROM DIGITAL LITERACY TO FLUENCY

A seismic shift in information can only lead to a necessary shift in the definition of literacy.

Literacy is not just about reading and writing anymore; its definition needs to be expanded. We know that literacy means competency and knowledge in a subject. It's the component of learning that requires someone to make meaning of something. As educators, we need to keep evolving as learners so we can be literate and competent in the new mediums of information entering our classrooms. Clint Lalonde reports in his article "Digital Fluency vs. Digital Literacy" that even the *2018 Horizon Report* emphasizes "the damage to student learning that can be done when faculty lack digital competency . . ."

To help educators build these competencies, we need to understand how the definition of literacy is evolving. We must practice transliteracy with our students and equip them to be fluent in all mediums of information, not just reading and writing. They need to understand narrative and bias in online text, searches, videos, images, and social media. They need to be able to tell a story—and tell it well—using one of these expanded and complex forms of information. And whether we like it or not, learning is happening online. Our students need new skills; they need to develop *new* literacies, and if we're going to get them ready for their future, we need to disrupt our definition of literacy.

What students need to develop is not just digital literacy but digital fluency. Students are very comfortable with technology and lack any fear in trying something out on a device. They jump in head-first and emerge ready to use the tool, which means they come to the table with a certain innate literacy. Don't believe me? Hand any five-year-old an iPhone and watch what happens.

As educators, if we **don't address the important idea of fluency, we might be doing students an injustice.** Fluency is the term that SHOULD be at the heart of everything we are talking about. It is where the **transfer of knowledge happens.** Kids get past the competency stage, apply the literacy they developed *without our help,* and transfer knowledge in becoming effective digital citizens and deep learners. This is the skill they must acquire with the help of knowledgeable educators.

A Closer Look at Fluency

Fluency is defined as the ability to express oneself easily, and in very simple terms, having fluency enables you to get to an end result: to have your message received and understood as it is intended. Fluency is what we need to shift our focus on with students and their use of technology for learning. **Fluency is different from literacy, because the former is simply making meaning of something, and the latter is the important concept of transfer of knowledge**—it's where digital savviness begins to grow from a seedling to a beautiful, blossoming tree.

I know **HOW TO USE** the tool, but also **WHY THIS TOOL** is the best one for my intended outcome.

For many years, I have come back to this definition posted on Socialens Blog that asserts:

"A literate person is perfectly capable of using the tools. They know *how* to use them and *what* to do with them, but the outcome is less likely to match their intention. It is not until that person reaches a level of fluency, however, that they are comfortable with *when* to use the tools to achieve the desired outcome and even *why* the tools they are using are likely to have the desired outcome at all."

This really encompasses the shift we need to make. We need to reframe our idea of digital knowledge. While we SHOULD pay attention to digital literacies when there are gaps, **the deep and important learning happens when we turn our focus to digital fluency.**

What I typically see in classrooms today...

Take online searching: Teachers know that students are literate enough to search on Google, so they allow them to search without regard for fluency. The question we should be asking as educators is: Are they *fluent* in a search? Do they know how to craft a search that will deliver to them a page of really meaningful and useful results? Can they distinguish between credible and non-credible sources? Do they have the fluency to evaluate the information the search produces? I promise you the answer is no in 98 percent of cases.

> # THERE IS A FLUENCY TO SEARCH, TO KNOW WHAT HAPPENS WHEN YOU ADD QUOTES, OR THE MINUS SYMBOL, OR KEYWORDS, AND HOW THIS ALL AFFECTS THE END RESULT.

> # THERE IS EVEN A DIGITAL FLUENCY IN UNDERSTANDING THE INTENDED MESSAGE (OR QUERY) YOU ARE DELIVERING TO GOOGLE.

Students need to understand how to effectively communicate and be digitally fluent enough to pick the right app for the right outcome or even app-smash some tools together to get the optimal effect. Telling students to pick any tool at the end of a unit to show their learning does not help them. They need to have the fluency to pick the right tool, and we do them a slight injustice by assuming they have it. **I believe focusing our efforts solely on literacy is short-sighted and incomplete. It is not literacy but fluency that should be our ultimate goal.**

As teachers, we also need to be digitally fluent.

But, here's the rub: **Educators who are not digitally literate and fluent can't teach what they don't know. And that is where a huge disconnect exists in our schools.** We must have fluency in these new mediums of information in order to get kids ready for a world of 2030 and beyond. We need to know which tools will garner the best information about students as learners so we can design more relevant instruction for their individual needs. We need to understand when technology can offer us real amplification opportunities for learning.

I often cringe when we only focus on digital literacy—we are not really equipping our students as we should. As we grow stronger in our understanding of technology and learning, it will become important for us to shift our focus from digital literacy to fluency. Educators in the 2020s must equip themselves to differentiate between the two concepts. They must understand why one may be even more important in school than the other. **Digital fluency is where the transfer of knowledge takes place; it is vitally important for learning.**

Help kids by changing the conversation at your school or district. Champion the idea of fluency while becoming fluent yourself! In addition, don't worry; the Infused Classroom has your back—the section on going from analog to digital will certainly help you develop those skills.

I need to be ready for a highly digital and connected future.

A QUICK LOOK ... TIME TO GET IN THE KNOW

Holly Clark

Education is full of buzzwords and acronyms—new ones pop up all the time. This section gives you an opportunity to learn (or review) important terms, acronyms, and concepts that characterize the Infused Classroom. Some of the relevant concepts in an Infused Classroom are represented with terms like Depth of Knowledge (DOK), the Four Cs, and ISTE Standards—however, these are much more than simple buzzwords and acronyms. These ideas require attention and careful study to make deep and meaningful progress in your thinking and practice. Based on solid pedagogy, these terms and ideas are important to familiarize yourself with.

This section ends with a look at digital citizenship so teachers can help students take a deeper look at the ways that their online persona contributes to their reputation and safety.

At the end of this section, you'll be tossing around buzzwords with the best of them! Better yet, your students will begin the journey to a mindful online presence.

GETTING TO KNOW
YOUR CHROMEBOOK

Congratulations! You have a Chromebook! Let's get to know this amazing device.

You have been given a Chromebook to use in your classroom with the intention that it will help students be more connected, collaborative, and creative. With this device, they will develop into more critical thinkers with open minds.

This is GREAT news because this transformational information device will enable you to change the focus of your classroom. Soon, your entire class will be student-focused and those *Aha!* moments will be flowing like water. Get ready to amplify teaching and learning in your classroom in ways that will blow your mind!

In order to work your teaching magic with the Chromebook, get to know the device, then understand the differences between it and other devices you are using.

Understanding
CHROMEBOOKS and
Digital Pedagogies

FUN FACT:
CHROMEBOOKS ARE NOW OUTSELLING MACBOOKS, AND THEY HAVE LONG SURPASSED THE IPAD FOR CLASSROOM USE.

A few features that make the Chromebook an awesome classroom tool:

It offers incredibly fast start-up time and takes less than eight seconds to boot up.

It has a super long battery life between eight to eleven hours, or an entire school day!

All work is saved to the cloud. You don't have to worry about students losing their work! Don't believe them if they say they did—and they will try.

You can work offline on the device, and when you get online, it automatically syncs all the information.

Work seamlessly with Google Apps for Education or G Suite, and if you love Microsoft, you can use that too!

Let's take a simple tour of your new Chromebook and check out the keyboard and trackpad functions:

Getting Started:

- To sign in to a Chromebook, you need a Google account. This is mandatory. Most likely, teachers and students will have school or district-issued Google accounts.

The Keyboard is a little bit different, so here is what you need to be in the know!

How do you turn it on? The power button is on the upper right-hand corner. (Mine is a lock button.) The entire line of top keys is different, though, and if you think of it as a searching toolbar, you will understand it better.

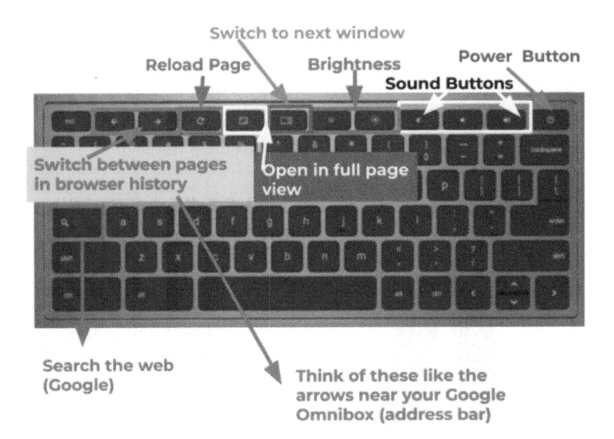

Switch to next window

Reload Page   Brightness   Power Button

Sound Buttons

Switch between pages in browser history

Open in full page view

Search the web (Google)

Think of these like the arrows near your Google Omnibox (address bar)

Common questions teachers and students have about some of the keyboard functions:

How Do I Take a Screenshot Now?

➔ **Full Screenshot ---> CTRL and Switcher button at top**

➔ **Partial Screenshot ---> CTRL, Shift and Switcher**

Where is the delete button?
ALT+Backspace

Where is the Caps lock?
ALT+Search

What is different about the trackpad? The trackpad is more sensitive than a click trackpad. It only needs a slight finger tap to respond to commands.

Click to select:
Tap once to select -or continue tap to drag an object

Right Click - Press or tap with two fingers

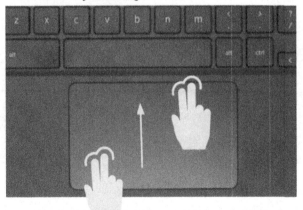

To Scroll: Two fingers up and down depending on which direction you want to go

To scroll between web pages (or use the arrow keys on top bar)

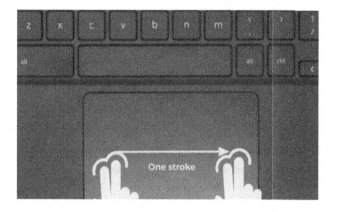

Swipe across with three fingers to move between tabs

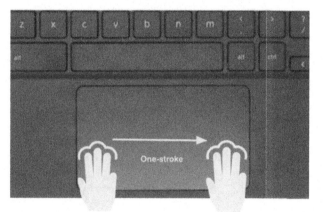

Chromebooks in your classroom will revolutionize the learning environment. The ideas in this book will help you craft experiences that are more powerful, meaningful, and transformational for your students.

A QUICK LOOK AT
DEPTH OF KNOWLEDGE (DOK)

With the changeover to Common Core, or Next Generation Science Standards (NGSS), Depth of Knowledge (DOK) has become almost common vernacular among teachers because the adoption of these new standards often corresponds to DOK levels.

However, not every teacher has had training in DOK, so we are going to take a moment to quickly look at what it is.

DOK was developed by Norman Webb around 1997 in an effort to understand the complexity of standardized test questions. To better grasp the purpose of DOK structures, Erik M. Francis's article for *ASCD In-Service Online* asserts,

"ESSENTIALLY, DEPTH OF KNOWLEDGE DESIGNATES HOW DEEPLY STUDENTS MUST KNOW, UNDERSTAND, AND BE AWARE OF WHAT THEY ARE LEARNING IN ORDER TO ATTAIN AND EXPLAIN ANSWERS, OUTCOMES, RESULTS, AND SOLUTIONS."

Most of us have come to learn about DOK from the widely publicized wheel shown here. This wheel is populated with verbs that describe the action employed by students at each level:

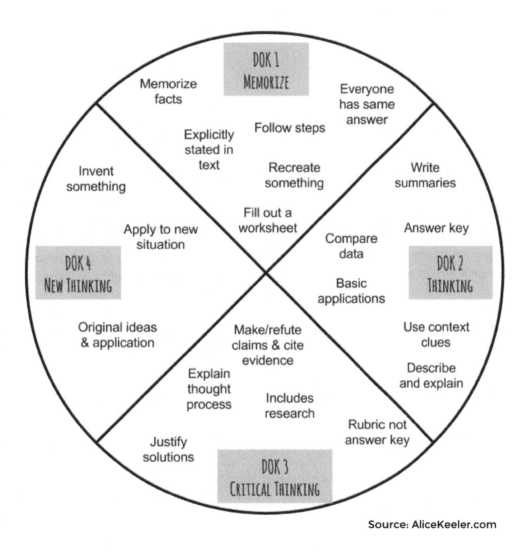

Source: AliceKeeler.com

Simply put, DOK is a way to understand **where classroom learning falls on a complexity scale.** As a guide, it helps teachers move students through all thinking and understanding levels so that learning experiences endure with maximum impact.

DOK LEVEL ONE

In this **knowledge acquisition** stage, students are doing basic tasks like spelling lists or filling in blanks on a worksheet. Although some information acquisition is needed, most seasoned teachers try to purposefully spend as little time here as possible. On the other hand, they might create learning environments where this happens organically as part of a larger project or inquiry unit.

DOK LEVEL TWO

This is about **knowledge application**. It might ask students to compare and contrast or even summarize information. A good example of this would be a six-word summary. While this task takes some level of critical thinking to find the perfect six words, its complexity is still at a DOK Level 2 because we have not quite entered the analysis stage, which comes next. Still, some analysis is required in the choosing of the six words. (DOK Level 3 seeks a more nuanced and sophisticated approach.)

Important: Most instruction I observe exists on the first two levels. For example, I saw one teacher who proudly had kids explaining the implications of a character's actions on the events in a novel, thinking she was at DOK Level 4. I worked with her to help her see how what she was asking did not require the type of analysis we are hoping to see in DOK Level 3. This teacher's lesson lived more at the **compare and contrast** and **cause and effect** level of DOK Level 2. It is not bad to be at any level; it is just important to fully understand the **progress of instruction** so you can help students get to deeper learning experiences.

In the art of teaching, a teacher weaves the DOK process throughout the lesson, allowing students to move in and out of levels as they work toward solving a problem or answering an inquiry. Students can also see their own learning progress by applying the DOK process. Teachers can even design a HyperDoc to ensure that all levels are reached during the learning experience. If designed correctly, the HyperDoc will provide students the opportunity to take charge of their own cognitive progress and learning acquisition.

What are the Four Cs, and why are they important to a Chromebook Infused Classroom? Let's take a quick look for a basic understanding of the concepts.

DOK LEVEL THREE

This stage is about knowledge analysis and might ask the student to take information from many sources and determine or guess how it might impact or change something being studied. It requires the **synthesis of information.** It might take a longer and more in-depth investigation to find a less obvious (or Google-able) answer or solution. I love this level as a place for productive collaboration between students so they go deeper into their analysis.

DOK LEVEL FOUR

The student is in the application stage but in a way that combines two components of learning and applies the result to a separate component. An example of this might be learning about the colonization of the United States and, based on lessons learned from this, producing a 'Strategy Manual' or PSA Video for people who will soon colonize Mars. It is in this application of information applied to a new situation that students experience the **transfer of knowledge** and will have a much higher rate of deep learning and understanding of the information.

A QUICK LOOK AT THE 4 CS

First, the four Cs that are essential components of a twenty-first century classroom are **Communication, Collaboration, Critical Thinking,** and **Creativity.**

Think of the four Cs as soft skills or character traits that enhance interpersonal capability and our success in working with other people. We need to incorporate these skills into our lessons, but they are more cultivated than graded. The skilled and intuitive educator finds a way to weave them into most lessons and purposefully adds opportunities for students to build these skills as part of classroom culture. We intentionally add them to the learning flow happening in the classroom.

You may have surmised that these types of skills will be very important for students once they hit the workforce. For this reason, including them in the early stages of student learning is vitally important to future success.

When Google asked the business community what skills were important in the workforce, the results affirm that the four Cs will play a crucial role in our students' future work lives.

So what does the future hold?

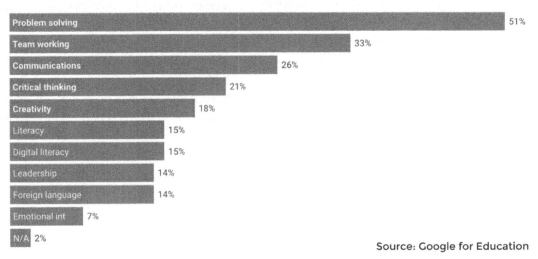

Skill	Percent
Problem solving	51%
Team working	33%
Communications	26%
Critical thinking	21%
Creativity	18%
Literacy	15%
Digital literacy	15%
Leadership	14%
Foreign language	14%
Emotional int	7%
N/A	2%

Source: Google for Education

Three Ways to Rethink Your Classroom with the Four Cs:

1 Have students work collaboratively as much as possible. Try pushing the boundaries of traditional learning by even allowing kids to work together on a final paper.

2 If they can Google an answer on a test, let them. Broaden the right-answer definition to include multiple perspectives and deeper thinking.

3 Allow students to ask questions **before** you begin a lesson or unit to activate curiosity. Create a culture of student-generated questions rather than always posing questions for students to answer.

What the Four Cs look like in the Classroom:

Communication

Articulately sharing thoughts and opinions in both verbal and written forms and knowing which medium would most effectively get a message across (digital fluency).

- Flipgrid
- Adobe Spark
- Book Creator
- Google Classroom

- Seesaw
- HyperDocs Lesson
- Podcasts

Collaboration

Working together toward a common goal.

Tip: Research has shown that collaboration works best in groups of three.

This can be with a local class or with other classrooms on a global scale.

This is best accomplished when students are sharing, discussing, and working together to solve a problem or grappling with a complex idea.

- Google Docs
- Book Creator
- Flipgrid
- HyperDocs Lesson
- Global Goals

- Flexible Seating

Critical Thinking

Being able to analyze, interpret, evaluate, and solve problems

Going beyond fact memorization, this skill can be applied outside the classroom.

- Google Docs
- Book Creator
- Flipgrid
- Geo Tools
- Problem-Based Learning
- Design Thinking
- Inquiry

- Sketchnoting
- Adobe Spark
- Solveintime.com

Creativity

Creating authentic products that are either remixed or an original idea turned into a learning artifact

Coming up with creative solutions to problems

Creative ways of demonstrating knowledge and trying new ways to accomplish a learning goal.

- Adobe Spark
- Google Slides
- Book Creator
- Seesaw

- Geo Tools
- Sketchnoting
- MakerSpaces

As you move through your journey of using the Chromebook for meaningful teaching and learning, consider adding these three Cs to your repertoire of good lesson design.

- **Consumption**–helping students develop the information literacy they need to be better online searchers and consumers of information

- **Curation**–helping students understand how to best organize information so they can find it again and use it for their own workflows

- **Curiosity**–allowing students the opportunity to ask questions and seek the answers for themselves

A QUICK LOOK AT ISTE STANDARDS

The International Society for Technology Educators (ISTE) is the gold standard for teachers wanting to modernize their instructional practices. The organization holds a yearly conference the last week of June in a different city in the United States. They also have state-based affiliates all around the US, and those affiliates have a conference each year as well.

> Check out the ISTE affiliate list **id.iste.org/connected/membership/affiliate-directory**

Some notable affiliates are listed below, and a quick Google search will get you to them:

- TCEA in Texas
- CUE in California
- IDEA in Illinois
- MACUL in Michigan
- NETA in Nebraska
- InnEdCO in Colorado

And who wouldn't want to go to HSTE in Hawaii?

To help teachers understand the needs of their learners and pursue their own professional growth, ISTE has established standards for Students, Educators, Educational Leaders, Coaches, Computational Thinker Educators, and Computer Science Educators. All of these have their own standards.

> You can find them at **iste.org/standards**

ISTE standards give teachers a reliable reference point for curriculum based on the ideas and skills ISTE has determined are valuable for students.

It is important to have these open on your computer as you begin to think about tasks students will be doing as part of the learning process and make sure you address at least three as you help facilitate learning.

For our purposes, we are going to just look at the ISTE standards for students covered in this graphic by expert sketchnoter Sylvia Duckworth:

Questions to Ask Yourself As You Begin Using the ISTE Student Standards:

- Are my students meeting these standards?
- How can I revamp a unit to give students more opportunities to meet the standards?
- Are there one or two standards I can focus on this year that will help me rethink instruction in my classroom?

Since our state and Common Core Standards have often not kept up with modern teaching needs, the ISTE Standards are an invaluable resource for any teachers wanting to move their instruction into more student-centered learning.

GETTING TO KNOW
DIGITAL CITIZENSHIP

Now that we have gotten to know the vocabulary the modern educator uses, it is now time to focus on how modern students can stay safe online. Hopefully, this will help keep our students from acting inappropriately online.

Digital citizenship is not a one-time discussion; it's an ongoing process that must be taught to all grade levels and all stakeholders. No matter how we feel about social media as adults, our students don't know a time when it did not exist. The problem is that things are changing so rapidly that keeping up to date with trends is difficult. Everyone must develop an understanding of the role digital citizenship plays in our everyday lives. So much goes into being a digital citizen, from taking photos of others to knowing appropriate online sharing practices.

Without any guidelines or structure, our students can get in a lot of trouble online and on social media. Armed with a concrete plan for teaching about appropriate use, you can guide your students to become better digital citizens who will learn how to build their digital presence in a positive and productive way.

Create an Acceptable Use Policy WITH Your Students—Give Them a Voice

Every September we pass out the obligatory Acceptable Use Policies (AUP) with little thought to what they include. We rarely cover the contents with students or parents. This is not enough to create responsible digital citizens! Instead, the first five days of a school term should be a time for a rich, in-depth discussion about online safety and responsibility. Get the students involved by beginning the discussion with a framework of questions that guide the process and write a classroom AUP together. When you involve students, they will surprise you with their ability to understand the choices behind their digital interactions. Stronger, more active, student voice equals greater student buy-in.

For this discussion, think about digital citizenship in a broader sense—not just at school but also at home and in transit. A rich discussion should include these and other components:

Who is responsible for the technology
or the devices you use—what does that entail?

Who is in charge of accounts,
and where do they keep the passwords?

Discuss the idea of password literacies:
knowing how to make and find them again when needed.

Talk about personalizing devices.
Can students insert any background, home screen, and profile images they want?

What will be the limits
on pictures and movies?

When can they use social media
for communicating with others?

What are the consequences
of off-task behavior in class?

What are the limits on personal work
on a device?

Who is responsible
for keeping devices charged?

Talk about respecting parents' rules
and why kids have to power down at a certain point.

We help create our **EXPECTATIONS** as we use the devices

We understand nothing is **PRIVATE** and we are learning about data privacy

We understand we are creating our personal **BRANDS**

We effectively **COMMUNICATE** and understand how to **BE KIND** online

Take a Dive into "Online Privacy"

It is essential that we teach our students that *nothing* they do online is *ever* private. Social media sites such as Facebook have created a false sense of security for our students and lured them into believing that privacy settings protect them. It is crucial that they understand what "digital" means. This is not the diary under their bed. On the contrary, it is the diary under everyone's bed! Everyone's digital life is easily reproducible and shareable to audiences around the globe. Young people can be naive about their vulnerability. Ask your students how many friends they have on Snapchat, and you will see that they are sharing things with hundreds of "friends" they don't really know. These friends can easily take screenshots of posts and re-share them with an unknown network of people. Consider demonstrating "social media cleanups" and having the students complete them for their Snapchat and Instagram accounts as a possible homework assignment. Reflecting on this cleanup effort will surely open the door to some important conversations.

Understanding Personal Identity—Students' Personal Brand and Reputation

Students need to understand that everything they post will become part of the online impression they make, or their "personal brand." To begin this discussion, have the students google themselves or a well-known public figure. Develop a discussion around the results and ask the students to share what they found. Were the results positive, negative, or neutral? If we put all the results together, what does this tell us about their digital footprint?

Digital Communication

Delve into the idea of appropriate digital communication. Digital interactions can quickly become a sticky issue with some students, especially if they all have the same device access. Students with iPads may want to use iMessage to work together during class, ask their teacher questions after school hours, and communicate with their work groups after school. This type of collaboration is powerful until someone misuses it. Is it appropriate to text your teacher a question? Should you use Twitter to carry on a private conversation? All of these questions need to be addressed early in the year, and the answers **must comply with school and district policies.** Discuss this topic and set clear guidelines that are not open to misunderstanding. Just as we passed notes in class, students today will find a way to pass digital notes. We need to be prepared for that, and these discussions will make a good starting point.

Digital Etiquette

Thanks to the abundance of devices in our lives, there are now more cameras in any given classroom than there are people. Having a discussion about photos and digital etiquette is now an essential component of any device-infused classroom. Given that parent release should have already been obtained, it is imperative to **address student-to-student permission.** Our students need to learn that they cannot take a picture or video of someone and post it online without obtaining approval. As students begin to share more media projects with the world, it is imperative that they follow certain guidelines. For fun and to hit the lesson home even more, students should have pseudo release forms ready for the other students to sign. This will serve to reinforce how important posting someone else's photos is to online privacy and reputation. Develop a shared vocabulary around etiquette and taking photos with students.

Digital citizenship lessons help lay the groundwork for a productive and positive year. It will clarify acceptable online communication. Starting the year off building awareness is the foundation to healthy and positive student digital identities, and discussing responsible behavior must be embedded into classroom culture.

THE
CHROMEBOOK
INFUSED
CLASSROOM

Holly Clark

Welcome to the opportunity to focus on your own deep learning and take time to reflect. There are fewer instructions and explicit learning ideas; instead, it is a time to carefully consider your own teaching and learning mindset—to push yourself and your practice. It provides a space to think about how your classroom environment and pedagogy are impacting your learners and maybe even their future success.

Teaching in a Chromebook Infused Classroom requires a definitive change in mindset and practice, and this new way of thinking is covered in this section. There is a detailed yet simple framework that will help you make changes in your classroom by putting student thinking and understanding at the forefront. No look into an Infused Classroom would be complete without examining critical concepts like the importance of tech in providing true equity and access to our students. Also—and this is crucial—educators need to rethink the traditional model of delivering instruction and begin to make the journey toward a more student-centered learning environment where student voice is honored. With that in mind, this section provides insight to help make this happen. Get ready for the seismic shift that will bring student engagement and learning to life!

THE INFUSED CLASSROOM FRAMEWORK
FOR EFFECTIVE TECHNOLOGY INTEGRATION

*Note: This article may look familiar as parts are taken from *The Google Infused Classroom* book, which makes a great companion resource. This review is helpful because it is foundational to our goals with Chromebooks.

Effective Technology Integration

Three core ideas are essential to an Infused Classroom: making thinking visible, giving every student a voice, and allowing students to share their work.

The purpose of this book is to help teachers think differently about how they use Chromebooks. We must transition beyond analog and teach digital. As a starting point, ask the following questions:

1. How can I make student thinking visible?

2. How can I use technology to hear from all students in the class and allow them to tell me where they are in the learning process?

3. How can I enable students to actively share their work (because we know they learn best from each other—more on this later)?

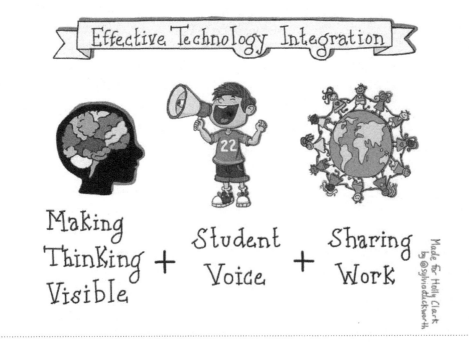

Making Thinking (and Learning) Visible

When students are allowed to use technology to write papers or take notes, it can certainly make their lives easier. On the other hand, replacing pen and paper with technology doesn't equate to making real advances in the way we use technology in schools. The goal is to ensure that we're using technology in ways that help students make greater gains in their academic growth and **also help us understand where they are in their learning process.** This way, we can make real-time changes in our instruction to better meet their needs as INDIVIDUAL learners. In order to do that, student thinking and learning must be visible to us—and to them.

In the past, it was difficult to help our students visualize their own thinking because we didn't have time to hear from all students and listen to their reflections. Students can't come one-by-one to our desks or conferencing areas; it requires too much labor and time. Thanks to today's technology, though, getting inside our students' heads—and finding out what they know and don't know—is easier than ever.

We can ask students to reveal their learning insights by offering the use of apps that enable them to articulate and record their thinking, ideas, and experiences. This is especially important because at the foundation of all good cognitive learning is the idea that we must teach our students **how to think about thinking (metacognition).**

To understand how students learn best, we must first make their thinking visible by using "thinking routines," or methods for questioning the learning process. In their book *Making Thinking Visible,* authors Ron Ritchhart, Mark Church, and Karin Morrison explain that thinking routines uncover the root of the thinking process. This key thinking routine from their book shows a way to monitor change or progress in student thinking:

Access some great thinking routines here:
bit.ly/ChromebookThinking

Thinking routines like the one above remind us that learning is not a product but a **process** of understanding.

Metacognitive processes like these must be woven into the very fabric of our classrooms so that students intuitively activate them to make connections and deepen their understanding.

As we progress through this book, we will talk about the ways to put student thinking into practice in a Chromebook Infused Classroom.

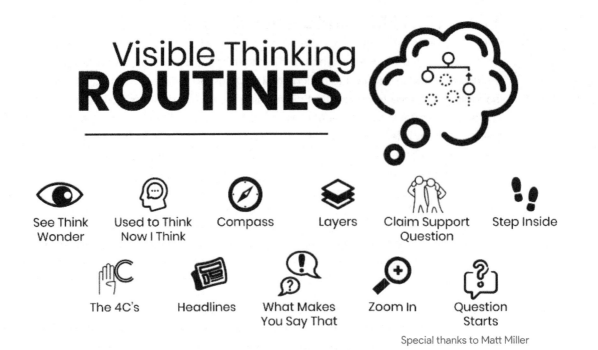

Visible Thinking ROUTINES

See Think Wonder

Used to Think Now I Think

Compass

Layers

Claim Support Question

Step Inside

The 4C's

Headlines

What Makes You Say That

Zoom In

Question Starts

Special thanks to Matt Miller

Student Voice

Think back to when you were a student. There were probably about four or five of your peers who always raised their hands first to answer any question. As a result, your teacher heard from these eager students frequently but had limited information about where the rest of the students in the class were in the learning process. Likewise, maybe our teachers would have us respond to questions by writing the answers on a piece of paper then place the paper with the answers face-down, pass them forward, and sit quietly as they were collected. It was as if we were sharing top-secret information only our teacher could read. Days would pass before we received feedback, and by the time the teacher knew if we understood the lesson, class was long over. Most students would have lost interest in the subject by then. Sadly, even the interval she spent collecting the papers resulted in lost learning time.

Beyond the obvious problem of getting everyone's active participation, the tools traditionally used to gather information about student learning, like fill-in-the-blank and multiple-choice questions, reveal very little about **how** students come to their conclusions or about **what** they really understand.

Thankfully, today's technology and tools have changed all that! With technology, we can now ask questions and hear from every child in the room—even the ones who are too shy or too intimidated to answer out loud. Now with Chromebooks, we accomplish this task in as little as two minutes—a fraction of the time used in previous information-gathering.

If you aren't hearing from every student in your class during crucial learning segments, you may not be using technology to its full capacity—but you can! For example, with an app like Socrative (socrative.com), you can ask a "Quick Question" from the Launchpad. Students enter your virtual classroom and quickly respond to the prompt. As the responses populate on the screen, you can easily ascertain **what the students have learned and where some understanding may still be lacking.** With this information, you can adjust your lesson in real time based on your students' individual needs.

Sharing Student Work

Technology can significantly upgrade student learning. Take sharing student work, for example. By incorporating visual thinking apps like Padlet (padlet.com), Socrative, and SeeSaw (web.seesaw.me) into this process, students can watch their peers' responses come in, compare their answers, make adjustments to incorrect thinking and maybe even learn something from the posted answers. It's during this sharing process that students access metacognition: they are thinking **about** their thinking.

We realize traditional teaching methods often discourage students from seeing one another's answers, but shared work is actually a useful resource. The foundational educational theory of *constructivism* asserts that people actually build their knowledge and meaning from their experiences. In short, **students learn best from one another,** and seeing another student's answers can often result in important lightbulb moments.

Additionally, students want to put their best foot forward when they know their work will be seen by peers instead of just their teacher. You'll notice that when your students know their work will be shared with the class, the school, or even with the world online, they will begin taking the time to construct more critical and carefully considered responses.

Employing the three techniques of making thinking visible, using technology to hear from every student, and allowing students to share their work affects student growth in a way that **empowers them to understand how they learn.** In effect, they learn *about* learning. When we combine these techniques with student-created demonstrations of learning to reflect on the process, that's when the magic really happens. Technology becomes something more than a word processor or powerful internet searcher—it amplifies the learning process.

> **NOTE:** This framework also gives students greater self-advocacy to pursue learning that best suits their learning needs, and it can help shift the teacher to more of a facilitator's role, which is more fitting in today's classroom.

THE TWELVE COMPONENTS OF AN INFUSED CLASSROOM

These components are not in order of importance because every aspect of The Infused Classroom is integral to all the others. This concept is driven by interdependence. All components are used in equal measure. One without the other is incomplete.

Often when people talk about The Infused Classroom, they think it's only about the infusion of technology and pedagogy. While we seek to improve by infusing the classroom with great teaching and learning in this area, it is so much more! Let's take a look at the twelve essential components of an Infused Classroom:

FLEXIBLE

1 A classroom that offers unique space and seating for learning experiences. It is a place that is not only arranged for movement and collaboration but also one where the teacher does NOT believe a classroom is organized to be tied to EVERY standard. The atmosphere honors diverse learning styles and diversity of thought. These classrooms still have structure, but they consider the individual and alternate routes to learning.

INFORMATION-RICH

2 This classroom has access to multiple devices, collaboration, information, and a larger learning community.

COLLABORATIVE

3 Students work together to take learning and construction of knowledge to new heights. Metaphorically, classroom walls are torn down, and the doors are always open so that students can work with classrooms in other geographical locations. They can also connect with experts who might be able to better help them make their own meaning of ideas and content.

DIFFERENTIATED

4

Different resources for multiple learning styles are provided to meet the needs of a diverse group of learners. In the classroom, each student has distinct access points that honor the learner where they are.

INQUIRY-DRIVEN

5

Student curiosity plays a central role in the Infused Classroom. As Trevor Mackenzie, author of *Dive into Inquiry* asserts: "Inquiry-driven learning proposes that questions and student interest can be the best indicators of student success. It honors that a learner's inquiry and curiosity should be as highly regarded as content."

CREATIVE

6

In his influential book *Educated By Design*, author Michael Cohen advocates for creativity in learning: ". . . a creative classroom is a space where students can research, explore and attempt to solve interesting problems that they care about. Learners in this environment seek out the unknown, embrace failure, and believe that the best solutions are achieved through collaboration and an empathetic lens."

CONNECTED

7

Learning has no geographical limits. Students engage in authentic learning, inquiry, and real-life situations. Extending beyond a classroom's physical walls opens up the entire world by enabling students to seek learning around the globe. A connected classroom allows students to explore outside their physical surroundings and connects them with experts everywhere.

PERSONALIZED

8

More than giving students choice in their assessments, it's about honoring the individual and developing passions. David Price emphasizes this idea in his book *Open*, advocating for "[the] need to understand how people learn when they have a choice and bring that [desire] into places where they are required to learn."

MINDFUL AND EMPATHETIC

9 The classroom should be a safe and open atmosphere, empathetic and compassionate toward diverse ideas, learning styles, entry points, experiences and the uniqueness of an individual's story. We need a balanced perspective to understand the whole person—and to be mindful that diversity of thought exists beyond our own experiences.

INCLUSIVE

10 It is important for classrooms to honor each student's unique perspective and contribution. This includes regard for learning differences and an appreciation for cultural, racial, gender, and LGBTQ diversity. Our teaching must embrace *sawubona*, a Zulu term of respect meaning "I see you; I honor who you are in this world" so that each student feels safe and respected.

MOVEMENT

11 The Infused Classroom should be bustling with movement, engaging discussion, and hands-on activity that get oxygen to the brain so that learning can be solidified. Learners need to move around and get away from their desks and construct knowledge without confinement to a rigid structure. Find a way to add activities to a lesson that gets kids moving.

STUDENT-DRIVEN

12 Students take agency over their learning. They set their own learning goals, keep track of their learning journey, and understand which tools will help them effectively demonstrate their new knowledge. Learners are encouraged to ask relevant, complex questions about a topic, and resources are available to help them find answers. They reflect on their learning and are constantly activating their own curiosities.

The Infused Classroom honors the student, the experience, and the time period.

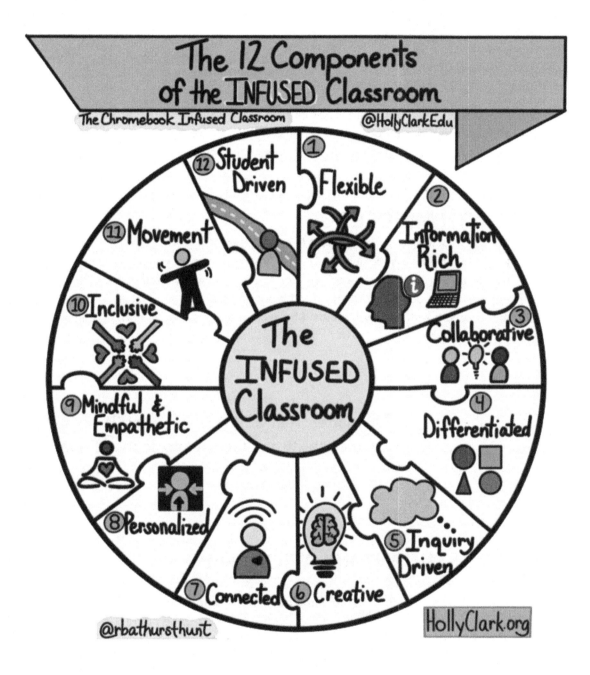

THE INFUSED TEACHER

Like the components of a Chromebook Infused Classroom, no single quality of an Infused Teacher is more important than another; instead, together they make up the whole package needed to be a teacher in this age of information and monumental change.

GROWTH MINDSET

Educators with a growth mindset live in a state of optimism. They are life-long learners, always looking for ways to improve, and they view failure as a necessary learning experience. They don't believe brains and talent are all that are needed to succeed but that hard work and learning are just as important. Teachers with a growth mindset have an infectious love of learning and a can-do attitude.

> No matter what your ability is, effort is what ignites that ability and turns it into accomplishment.
>
> —Carol Dweck

BUILDS STUDENT RELATIONSHIPS

The number one predictor of student success is often the relationship a student has with a teacher. **Classrooms need to be safe social and emotional spaces for kids.** Get to know your students personally. Understand their family situations and their challenges and interests so that students see you as an advocate, more interested in them as human beings than in their classroom achievement. **A simple smile, a word of encouragement, or a caring gesture can go much farther than feedback on content.** Maybe put down the red pen and put on a smile if you want to see student scores increase.

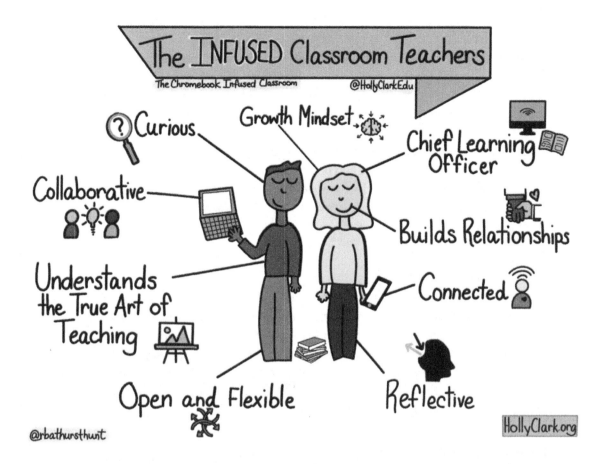

CHIEF LEARNING OFFICER

Teachers need to think of themselves as learners first. They stay current with education books and blogs and actively apply innovations happening globally to the learning process in their own classrooms. Their online connections help fuel their learning and inspire their craft.

CONNECTED

In this day and age, connection to other educators is the key to learning and developing as a professional. No teacher can get everything he or she needs from school PD. Fortunately, social media provides a great way to quickly build a tribe of educators, both local and global, who help you grow and reflect on learning. Find a solid one hundred teachers to follow on Twitter or Instagram, try out some of their methods, provide feedback, and share some observations of your own to get the most out of your online Professional Learning Network (PLN). Try EdSpace.live and check out The Infused Classroom Channel to stay up-to-date with all things Infused.

REFLECTIVE

Keep a journal about students and how they respond to the learning environment, material, collaborative work, and a variety of activities. From there, you can determine which ideas and strategies work best for each student and how you can modify your practice to meet all students' needs. My friend Lisa Highfill says it best: "A reflective teacher is one who 'studies' students as they learn, who then takes that information to form ideas about how they learn best, how your lesson fits their needs, and how they can revise/edit to make it more effective. **When you are reflective and studying your students, you can see what they need; you know their needs and design learning for them—not for you or a test.**"

OPEN AND FLEXIBLE

Infused Teachers never consider their understanding or expertise to be static or immovable, even if they are education veterans. They openly welcome the diversity of individual student stories and infuse that into the class story. **They are flexible and want students to pursue more authentic, inquiry-based, and relevant learning instead of stressing over the idea that not all standards can be met because they never can.** Students need educators who are open to meeting student needs with new ways of learning.

UNDERSTANDS THE TRUE ART OF TEACHING

As a teacher, you see individual distinctions and you are looking for patterns. To find those patterns, however, you must invest in each student's personal story. With investment in your students' stories, it's easier to make connections and predictions about what a student might need to progress. You introduce the 'color' or concepts the students need to spark curiosity and experience a transfer of knowledge—that sweet spot where the learning truly sticks. You are at ease living in a continually changing and evolving landscape, making quick decisions and connections. Reflecting along the way, you look at the big learning picture and what other elements might need to be incorporated. **You view each class as a unique work of art that combines many separate and individual pieces to form something truly illuminating.** You understand that all those parts come together to form a complete picture, like a beautiful mosaic.

COLLABORATIVE

Spending face-to-face time working with other teachers and educators is key to improving your practice. Gone are the isolating days of just teaching with your classroom door closed. Actively look for and find a colleague you respect and visit their classroom as often as you can. **Work collaboratively to create the best environment for your students, invite other teachers to see what you are building, and ask for feedback.**

CURIOUS

Curiosity might just be the crucial C that leads to lifelong success, and curiosity is especially important in this time of such a dramatic shift in the flow of information. Curiosity will augment readiness for change. **Curious teachers can instill a sense of curiosity in their students, who will need guidance in asking relevant questions and making meaning of the information they discover.** Teachers do not need to always be experts; they can learn and grow alongside their students. This changes the nature of the teacher and student relationship from one of authority and subordinates to a collaborative team on the road to discovery!

The Infused Teacher knows great teaching is both art and science, focused on all learners in the classroom. Your unique enthusiasm and personality become an integral part of learning. As you learn and try new methods, you become more skilled—but you never arrive at perfection. Focus on student development and grow comfortable with how each learner might need a different concept, color, or entry point into and throughout the learning. Learn to view a room full of curious learners as a work of art.

EQUITY IN THE INFUSED CLASSROOM: A CLOSER LOOK AT TECHQUITY

Co-written with Ken Shelton (kennethshelton.net)

As more and more students get devices such as Chromebooks in their hands, education begins putting one foot forward toward more **equitable digital access** to both information and more relevant learning experiences. For students who might not have had the same opportunities at home, this can be a great equalizer, but we must take this opportunity one step further and use technology to provide a more relevant and inclusive classroom curriculum.

Ken has used the term "techquity" to describe the dynamic combination of access to technology and the rich information that brings greater equity to all students irrespective of race, gender, ethnicity, or socioeconomic status. While having the technology is a crucial first step, it can fall short of the kind of learning that needs to happen now that students have access to information never before seen in human history.

The idea of classrooms employing more devices, and thus gaining more access, is always great news. But it's about the POWER of the device to supercharge learning. Real techquity exists when we begin to merge the use of educational technologies with culturally responsive and relevant learning experiences to support student development of essential skills. Techquity happens when these key ingredients exist in a learning environment: **access**, **culturally relevant learning experiences**, and **inclusivity**.

How can we make sure techquity is happening and that our students have a chance to learn in ways that resonate with their own life experiences? This might require a shift in thinking to consider the extensive information students now have access to that might not be covered in traditional texts.

Teachers may not know this, but when dominant culture stories are read as a class, there is a high likelihood that students of color can experience varying degrees of trauma. They grow uncomfortable; they may shut down and will likely lose interest in the reading. As educators we want to avoid this type of learner trauma as it can have lasting effects. An antiquated and non-inclusive approach to literature study often leads to kids who tell their teachers, "I hate reading." We should strive to be receptive in our work and design learning. Our support of a culturally responsive and relevant experience reduces the likelihood of trauma and is more reflective of our diverse and changing world.

Let's take the traditional method of literature study in secondary grades as an example. For decades, we have drawn from novels like *The Outsiders* and *To Kill a Mockingbird* to teach lessons about struggle, racism, and redemption. We have often taught these novels as a whole-class study, understanding and centering the learning experience around the perspective of the dominant culture. Typically, these literature units are from the perspective of white privilege and its trials and tribulations. This can impact students of color in ways educators might not have considered. The perspective may leave them feeling marginalized or left out. Today, though, we can provide students with access to a variety of titles from vastly different social, racial, cultural, and ethnic perspectives. We can also include authors like Sandra Cisneros or Toni Morrison and research more inclusive narrative forms, like poetry and song, to augment perspective and voice.

Each year two educators Scott Bayer (@Lyricalswordz) & Joel Garza (@JoelRGarza), make a goal of introducing readers to authors from a variety of genres, backgrounds, and experiences. They also hope to get these texts into classrooms by designing a HyperDoc for each that can serve this purpose.

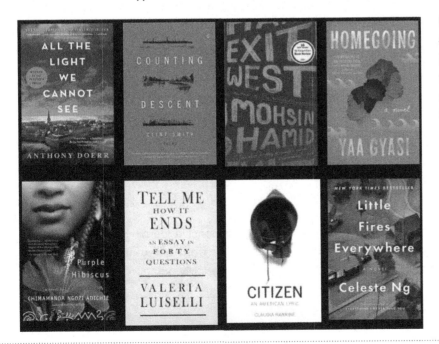

Follow their journey on #TheBookChat for upcoming books and chats around the books they choose. Here are some example titles from 2019-2020.

CHROMEBOOKS
AND THEIR ROLE IN TECHQUITY

Access

Chromebooks democratize access for all students by making access and relevant teaching materials easier to find and in a more cost-effective and equitable manner.

Universal access to information provides students with a learning environment specifically designed for learning from multiple viewpoints. In this way, the learning can be more responsive to the needs of all learners and be the catalyst for deeper, more empathetic understanding of the diverse backgrounds that exist not only in the classroom but the world.

Relevance

Even better, we can design learning assessments that are strategically aligned with more inclusive goals and more responsive to individual abilities. For example, teachers may be unaware that a student has never seen a farm when they assign reading passages about farms. Background knowledge is a key indicator in reading success, so if a student is unfamiliar with a setting, consider how this might impact their overall comprehension and interest.

Inclusivity

Now that we have this incredible access through the Chromebook, how can we create more inclusive lessons and classrooms? In a Chromebook Infused Classroom, this can happen in many ways:

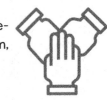

1 Provide students opportunities to work with experts from authentic and diverse backgrounds and include non-dominant culture representations in the learning.

2 Encourage and support students in a culturally responsive learning experience by gathering information and resources from different points of view on the same event or experience, especially points of view from marginalized people or communities.

3 Ensure that students have access to video-based platforms to connect to people with more background or experience on a particular topic.

4 Teach students how to conduct a well-executed Google search so that they are better at fact-checking possible fake news and biased stories.

5 Allow for the stories of people of color to be told. Look for those that exemplify strength, integrity, and resilience. Consider historical investigations from Howard Zinn and Malcolm Gladwell.

6 Support and encourage students with learning exceptionalities to use apps and resources that enable them to succeed in an environment free from penalty or stigma regarding their differences.

7 Create project-based learning that is aligned with students making real-life connections between the academic content and the local neighborhood, culture, and environment.

8 Instead of the teacher being in charge of the learning, encourage students to ask meaningful questions, thoughtfully investigate, challenge and form opinions on their own, and leave room and safety for these to not be aligned with the dominant culture.

With increased technology access, we can provide students with much more diverse information that includes multiple student perspectives. Chromebooks enable educators to offer more diverse fiction and non-fiction narratives that illuminate and celebrate previously marginalized voices and experiences, inspiring empathy and understanding.

Let's use Chromebooks to support a more relevant and inclusive classroom to make a lasting difference in *all* student learning.

TEN QUESTIONS TO ASK
WHEN USING A CHROMEBOOK

How can I use the Chromebook to **activate curiosity** before we begin a lesson?

How can students use the Chromebook to **access materials that are representative of different identities, backgrounds, and cultures**?

How can the Chromebook make the **learning more individual and student-centered**?

HYPERDOC OR BOOK CREATOR WOULD WORK HERE

Can I use the technology to enhance the learning experience by **making it more collaborative**? How can students work together on this project instead of alone?

Can the Chromebooks be used to **access different opinions and ideas outside the traditional text**?

How can I design learning assessments where students use the Chromebook to provide the teacher with real-time information and **make their thinking and learning visible?**

FLIPGRID WOULD
WORK HERE

Are all of my students showing their understanding in the same way? Is there a way for me to allow for **demonstrations of knowledge that are more student-centered** and meet the needs of each of their learning differences?

How is the Chromebook activity better than a worksheet or written response, like filling in a blank or regurgitating answers? If it's not, how can I use the Chromebook to **make the learning richer and more dynamic?**

SEESAW OR ADOBE
SPARK WOULD
WORK HERE

How can I use the Chromebooks to enable students to **experience learning outside of the four walls of the classroom?** Can we connect with another classroom on this particular learning outcome? Can we bring in an expert?

How can I bring in those learning tools that will help all students have the same access to information, and is there a tool that can help a **struggling learner have better access to the information**? What inclusive tools are out there?

TEN WAYS TO RETHINK THE DELIVERY MODEL OF INSTRUCTION

Bolded words are further explained in this book.

As we make the move to more student-centered classrooms, it means teachers have to find a way to spend less time at the front of the room. Here is a quick list of ten ways to help teachers shift their classroom role from deliverer of instruction to that of facilitator of learning.

1 Consider using a **HyperDoc:** a student-facing lesson that replaces the old delivery model of instruction through blended learning. More on this in the next section.

2 Take a look at the Digital Questions section that explains the **Question Formulation Technique (QFT)**, which will empower students to ask the questions that will drive their learning.

3 Consider learning more about the **Inquiry Method** of teaching with books like Trevor MacKenzie's *Dive into Inquiry* and *Inquiry Mindset*. Inquiry is when we allow *student interest* to drive instruction.

4 Give students the time and opportunity to **discuss and unpack** ideas on their own.

Develop **visible thinking routines** that allow students to delve into concepts with prompts like "What if?" or "I used to think . . . now I think . . ."

Implement the **hot-seat method**, where students sit on a 'hot seat' to answer questions from the point of view of a character, element, math equation, or whatever will allow deeper thinking around an idea.

Rearrange the chairs in your room into **groups of three**. This number allows for more dynamic collaborative groups as students discuss, unpack, deconstruct, and construct knowledge collaboratively.

Scaffold directions and instructions to help move from the traditional teaching model to student-driven learning.

Use a wide range of **checks for understanding** to assess where students are in their learning process. This knowledge will help enable them to have power over their learning.

Use a **Multimedia Text Set** (or exploration board) to give students a chance to activate their curiosity before a lesson. This is discussed in greater detail in the HyperDocs section of this book.

THE
CHROMEBOOK
INFUSED
STUDENT

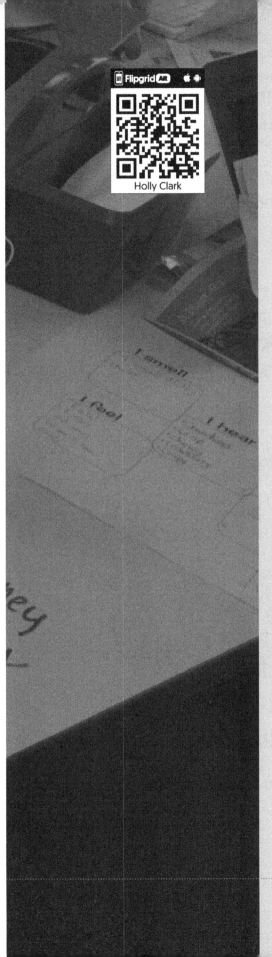

Holly Clark

As educators who have access to more and more technology in the classroom, we need to rethink the student role in learning. **Students need to see themselves as people in control of their own learning, not just passive receivers of information.**

Because teachers were most likely born BG—Before Google—we didn't see the power of networked learning in action as students, and we may only now be experiencing its power as adults. Our students are far more networked than we were at their age. If you're like me, you probably lived through an era where being online was a cool add-on to what we were already doing in the classroom. But today, the networking landscape is far different. **We can no longer view technology and its various devices as a nuisance or an obstacle to rich and reflective learning. Technology is essential, and it is here to stay.**

With that said, how do we teach in this new tech era? Many of us are unprepared to tackle this problem, so we turn to any resources we can get. Social media such as Twitter, Facebook, and Instagram have become indispensable assets for knowledge-thirsty teachers. In addition, while the online teaching and learning community has revolutionized teacher development, it is still difficult to sort through ideas to determine what would best meet our own professional needs and the needs of our students. **The Infused Classroom not only helps teachers rethink their approach to teaching and learning with technology, but it also turns our attention to the students and their needs in the age of networked learning.** Students with a computer have more than just access at their fingertips. They become active and engaged learners. They *direct* their learning instead of passively receiving it. This may be a difficult adjustment, but put away the Google Slides or PowerPoint and consider stepping back so students can take charge of their own learning process.

As we guide learners to take ownership of their learning in an access-rich classroom, four parts of the learning cycle shift dramatically to the forefront:

Instead of teachers asking what they can do with the technology, we need to ask what our *students* can do with the technology. This shift in thinking helps us begin to create more student-centered classrooms. To do this, learning should happen with this four-part cycle in mind. To help you better understand this cycle, each of the components of the Infused Classroom Student will be broken down and examples provided in the subsequent pages.

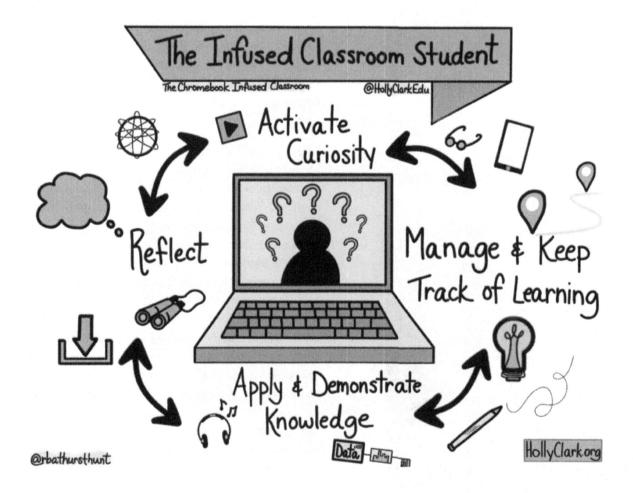

ACTIVATE CURIOSITY

Students are innately curious, and curiosity might just be the crucial C that leads to lifelong success. While teachers are very familiar with those building blocks of successful learning, the 4 Cs (critical thinking, collaboration, communication, and creativity), curiosity does not make the list. This is alarming because it may affect our readiness for such a dramatic shift in information. Without a foundation of curiosity, the other learning building blocks collapse. We have to activate and help students harness curiosity. Combining curiosity with technology can supercharge learning and transform many more young people into innovators and game-changers than ever before.

We have to ask ourselves some honest questions:

- Does my classroom foster curiosity?
- Do my students see a reward in asking questions?
- Are they simply looking to meet my expectations for a grade?

It is important to take some time to reflect on teaching practices and see if we might need to adjust it to encourage curiosity. Before diving in, first give students time to pique curiosity by exploring and asking their own questions about the content. Have them talk with other students about what they know by both comparing and augmenting their own ideas. Student interest is raised in this phase as they think about what they know and want to know and have time to collaborate with their peers about this.

How We Do This

- **Try using The Question Formulation Technique** rather than the students-will-be-able-to (SWBAT) formula of telling students what they will know at the completion of a unit. Even worse is writing the standards on the board. Instead, spark curiosity using The Question Formulation Technique. Begin by giving each student time to ask questions in a structured way. With this expectation, students learn to ask deeper and more meaningful questions, and each student participates. To learn more, visit **infused.link/rightquestion** or head to the digital questioning section in this book.

- **Try using a version of a HyperDoc** (hyperdocs.co) to create a one-stop digital resource with multiple sources that activate curiosity, known as a multimedia text set. For additional examples, check out the MMTS section (MultiMedia Text Sets) or start by looking at this example of a Text Set on refugees from Lisa Highfill and Scott Padway: **infused.link/refugee.** This design gives students time to explore the idea of refugees before the unit even begins, creating important background knowledge that helps them be more successful learners. More on HyperDocs later in this book.

➩ For more support, join the discussion in the Infused Classroom FB group: **facebook.com/groups/infusedclassroom**

MANAGE AND KEEP TRACK OF LEARNING

Before we begin any unit, we need to reach an important pedagogical goal during this exploratory time. Make sure that you have garnered an assessment of each student's prior knowledge so you can understand where students are at the start of a unit—even *after* they have activated curiosity.

You will use that information and compare it with where they are at the end of the unit. This data is what you will use to measure each student's growth over time. It is how you truly **personalize** education—by looking at a student's individual learning journey instead of measuring them all against the same *standardized* learning target.

To assess prior knowledge, try using Flipgrid (flipgrid.com):

- Ask students to tell you everything they know about an idea, topic, or subject before they begin. I like to ask students to do this alone first.

- After that, they can work with a partner to exchange ideas.

- Next, they use the reply button on their own video to discuss the information they gained by talking it out with a partner.

STEP TWO:
Manage and Keep Track of Learning

Students can now begin to take an active role in their learning journey. As students make their way through the learning cycle, whether by acquiring content, constructing knowledge, or taking part in inquiry, they need to learn to track and refer back to their learning progress. ISTE student standards are rich with reminders of this. These standards ask that students begin taking an active role in setting their own learning goals. According to the standards, "The Empowered Learner articulates and sets personal learning goals, develops strategies leveraging technology to achieve them, and reflects on the learning process itself to improve learning outcomes."

In this way, students watch as their knowledge builds. Later, they use this information as they apply and reflect on the learning. For this step, students gather their learning artifacts and their formative assessments and curate these in a useful application like Google Drive, Seesaw or Book Creator. This way, they have an idea of where they started, where they are at present, and how far they have progressed by the end. Along the way, a teacher facilitates the process of making their thinking and learning visible with periodic checks for understanding (I recommend Flipgrid for this.). Periodic reflection *during* the process will produce deeper reflection on the journey *at the end* of this process.

How We Do This
Students use their assessment of prior knowledge to begin to set their own learning goals, record them, and refer back to them as they reflect on their learning.

A great resource comes from the book *Developing Assessment-Capable Visible Learners*, where authors Frey, Hattie, and Fisher break down the learning journey into five distinct parts:

1. I know where I am going.
2. I have the tools for the journey.
3. I monitor my progress.
4. I recognize when I am ready for what's next.
5. I know what to do next.

Consider using tools like Book Creator (bookcreator.com) to keep track of the learning—both the goals and the individual artifacts—or have students write their goals in Google Keep or anywhere that's easy to refer back to.

APPLY AND DEMONSTRATE KNOWLEDGE

Next, students begin to take their learning and apply and demonstrate it. This is a very important part of any learning journey. To do this, students might create a learning artifact that demonstrates their understanding of the content. For deeper learning, students can take this new knowledge and apply it to something authentic or real-life such as a current event or different subject matter. **This deeper process, called "Transfer of Knowledge," is where learning begins to take root and is solidified.**

STEP THREE:
Apply and Demonstrate Knowledge

To ensure that students create meaningful demonstrations of learning, the methods they use must be multifaceted and layered. Thankfully, technology allows students to demonstrate their learning in authentic and rich ways. It provides us with the opportunity to hear from all students, uncover their thinking, visualize the steps they took and the applications they made, and understand the **metacognition** behind the experience.

Technology makes it possible to take something that was once one-dimensional, such as a poster, and layer it with student voice, explanations, and even virtual reality to bring their learning to life.

As a result, learning becomes much more meaningful and interesting in the process. Students are constructing knowledge, keeping a record of their journey, and showing their learning through a digitally rich product—when it best suits the learning goal. Please note: Sometimes pen and paper work fine here too.

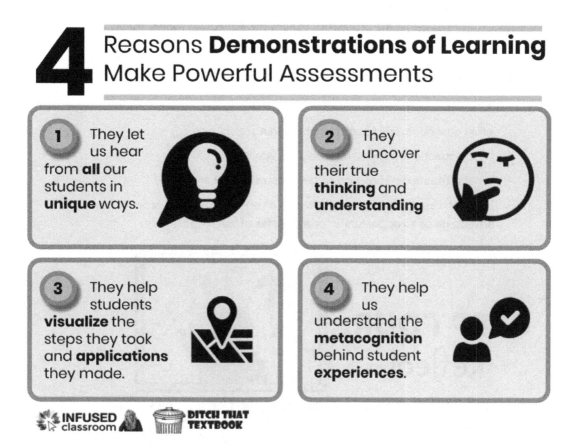

4 Reasons **Demonstrations of Learning** Make Powerful Assessments

1 They let us hear from **all** our students in **unique** ways.

2 They uncover their true **thinking** and **understanding**

3 They help students **visualize** the steps they took and **applications** they made.

4 They help us understand the **metacognition** behind student **experiences**.

INFUSED classroom   DITCH THAT TEXTBOOK

How We Do This

If we are asking for a digital artifact of learning, teachers could use something like Adobe Spark (spark.adobe.com), where students can take their learning and wrap it up in a media creation. Here is an example of an Adobe Spark Page from a fifth-grade writing assignment: **infused.link/adobesparkpost**

For more examples, visit this Wakelet collection: **infused.link/adobe**

REFLECT ON THEIR LEARNING JOURNEY

John Dewey says, "We do not learn from experience . . . we learn from *reflecting on experience*." At this point, students return to their learning journal (in something like Book Creator) to begin the process of reflection. Reflection allows students and teachers to understand and own the full learning process.

The learning should include all aspects of the experience:

- Where did I start?
- What questions did I have at the beginning?
- Which questions popped up along the way?
- What artifacts did I produce to demonstrate my learning?
- How can I apply that learning to a new or novel situation in order to take advantage of an opportunity for a transfer of learning?

STEP FOUR: Reflect

At this point, significant learning artifacts, along with explanations and a reflection, can be turned in for a grade. Here it is important to have students record their thinking so you can 'hear' the process. We know that if a student can tell what they have learned, chances are they learned it! This is much more insightful than a multiple-choice unit test.

A great way to implement reflection can be by using an app like Flipgrid, where students articulate in a video response what they have learned and how they have reached their learning goals. We know that students who passively receive information forget it. In reflection, active learners not only gain knowledge of content, but they cultivate curiosity in the process and keep that curiosity alive for their next learning experience.

The multifaceted use of technology changes the game in the classroom. Students can now have a more active role in their own learning, so we educators shift from expert to facilitator and guide. This way, the classroom becomes truly student-centered and personalized—a springboard for lifelong curiosity and deeper learning. After all, isn't that what we want for our students?

WE KNOW THAT IF A STUDENT CAN TELL WHAT THEY HAVE LEARNED, CHANCES ARE THEY LEARNED IT!

TAKING THE LEAP: GOING FROM ANALOG TO DIGITAL

Holly Clark

The goal in a Chromebook Infused Classroom is to take learning from **analog** to **digital**. It is *not* just for ease and speed. A digital platform provides data with a much broader scope, giving teachers greater insight into individualized student learning and growth. It also provides students greater agency in the learning process and more meaningful ownership over their work. It makes learning more powerful.

Before we begin thinking about this transition, we have to remember it's more than just going paperless. It's about using technology to amplify personalization, creativity, collaboration, critical thinking, communication, and problem-solving. We don't want to simply replace old tasks with new technology but make the tasks authentic and meaningful so students can develop the most important literacy of learning: learning itself.

With Chromebooks, we can now focus on the **process** of learning, rather than just the end product. You have been given Chromebooks in your classroom so that you can uncover the process, not just give online quizzes.

As we go through this section, you will notice ideas that include traditional classroom tasks, like reading and writing. But digital learning should bring these tasks to a place where learning is **amplified**. It becomes more targeted to individual student interest and incorporates the kind of collaboration that effectively unpacks complex ideas, which leads to richer learning experiences and true **construction of knowledge**.

In this stage, we look for ways to make student thinking and learning **visible**, which is covered in greater depth in the framework section of the book.

from **Analog** TO **Digital**

@monicaisabelmtz

Your Chromebook Infused Classroom should create conditions in which your students can develop as true learners. They need the ability to ask the big questions. They need information literacy in order to find and validate answers. Most importantly, students need to **learn how to learn**.

As you go through this new journey with the Chromebook, keep in mind that you are moving toward a focus on process rather than the end result for true twenty-first-century learning.

> Nothing could be more absurd than an experiment in which computers are placed in a classroom where nothing else is changed.
>
> —Seymour Papert

USE THE POWER OF SIMPLICITY
TO CHANGE YOUR CLASSROOM

In this section, we will look at how to go from analog to digital in meaningful and learning-centered ways. As teachers make this journey, though, remember these three words: Keep It Simple.

Technology in classrooms can stimulate teaching and learning but integrating technology is not always easy. For many reasons, teachers often don't opt for a technology-infused unit. Fear and discomfort can prevent teachers from incorporating this important resource into their classrooms. Some may not know where to start or don't know how to effectively use it. Others may even feel they don't have time to learn it. It can also be intimidating to teach Generation Z students how to use it.

How do we solve this? By keeping it simple.
Start small. Find a few apps that are easier to integrate and students can use on the fly without too much instruction on your part. Look for tools that will provide rich information about student learning and growth that are also easy to use and integrate in class. We want to find tools that are more intuitive and accessible for student use, even without an expert's instruction.

To do this, we need to develop a "tool belt" of apps that can **more effectively** get at student thinking. This can be tricky—we don't need to search for tools that simply replace what we are already doing in the classroom. Instead, technology helps us craft a learning environment to better understand the content and give students a platform to demonstrate learning. We also want student learning to be a rich and evolving process. Students should take learning with them, not just regurgitate information and then move on.

> Simplicity is the ultimate sophistication.
> —**Leonardo Da Vinci**

To help us better understand, let's unpack an example:

In California, all fourth graders learn about The California Missions. They were twenty-one outposts constructed by Spanish explorers to house military troops and Franciscan missionaries. This action helped colonize the territory and convert its native inhabitants to Christianity. (It didn't all go down this nicely, but for this example, we won't go into the injustices that were used to build the state of California.)

Before technology, the standard unit project required students to build a miniature replica of a mission. Parents got involved, and these projects became so elaborate that it could take months to build them. In the end, building these replicas became the focus of the lesson, with little true learning and understanding value. Instead of the essential question being about what impact colonization had on a region or the Spanish had on the growth of California, this task was eclipsed by the process of making a replica mission.

When some California schools received devices, teachers often replaced replica mission building with an assigned movie about the project. It infused a 'cool factor,' but technology still did not enhance the learning or help students understand the implications of colonization. Technology should be a **tool** for deeper learning and not the focus of the lesson.

So how might teachers use technology more effectively?

We want to aim for a SIMPLE but powerful infusion of technology in this case. The teacher could create a Flipgrid (flipgrid.com) for this. The Grid would be "The California Missions," and the topics might be *The Players, Colonize Mars,* and *Lesson Learned.*

For *The Players*, students could assume the role of someone living in California during the late 1700s, research a person, and record a segment explaining that person's perspective on colonization. The grid could have priests (even Father Junipero Serra, himself), soldiers, the Spanish king, natives—anyone involved in building or visiting the missions during this time period. On this grid, students could research the person they chose and record a narrative, detailing their experience and feelings—not just by reading from notes, but by taking the perspective of the chosen character. In character, students could then reply to each other, exploring empathy for people in the past, connecting with events, and asking real questions about the value of the Spanish missions. Later, to get at a true transfer of knowledge, students could apply their learning to other situations and construct a grid in which, still in their eighteenth-century character, they could give advice to people who want to colonize Mars today.

An example of the California Missions Grid from the teacher's point of view in Flipgrid—simple, yet requiring sophisticated learning.

While the technology is simple, the learning is complex. This project includes research, recall, elevator pitches, writing, and understanding. It requires that students construct knowledge and apply it to a different situation. In this case, it's the colonization of Mars, which could actually be happening by the time they graduate from college!

The final step—some might argue, the most important—might be called *Lessons Learned*. In this step, students reflect on how their character's actions affected other people and what this information can teach us about the implications of colonization or regional growth in the process.

While an example for California fourth-grade teachers, this lesson can be easily applied to all subjects. Begin by nailing down the essential questions, enduring understandings and transfer of knowledge students should have at the end of your unit. After that, find the tech tool that best enables you to connect with their thinking and understanding. This way, the journey is simple, but the learning is profound.

With simplicity in mind, we use technology to assess student learning and understanding, to include every student, and to enable all students to share their learning, experiencing a **transfer of knowledge**. There is time in every classroom for more multi-level projects, but our job as teachers is to know where our students are in the learning process and help them progress on their individual journey of understanding. If used right, technology can make this process that easy *and* profound.

As teachers make the journey with Chromebooks, keep the word **simplicity** at the forefront. While this example included Flipgrid, consider Google Slides, Padlet, Adobe Spark, Book Creator and Seesaw. (See "Meet the Tools" for more information on these apps.) These simple tools can easily improve teaching and learning in the classroom. When you begin to think that technology takes too much time or requires an elaborate pre-designed task, just remember it's *simply* not true.

DIGITAL ASSESSMENTS:
UNCOVERING THE GENIUS IN EVERY CHILD

> We now have extensive evidence that highlights the potential of brains and bodies to change, and that calls into question the myth of 'Natural Genius' and 'Giftedness.' Once we know that brains and people can achieve almost anything, it should lead us to think of human potential— and institutions of learning— entirely differently.
>
> —Jo Boaler

A teacher with Chromebooks can revolutionize the assessment process.

With access to these devices, assessments can evolve and provide a much richer picture of student learning and growth. It starts by re-examining how we capture true knowledge and understanding from students. Up to this point, educators have had very few ways to assess their students, so they relied on memorization and recall. But as Nancy Frey, John Hattie, and Douglas Fisher state in their book *Defining Assessment-Capable Visible Learners*, "Memorization and recall have their place in the cycle of learning, but rarely at the start, and certainly not at the end of learning."

Given that idea, what is a better assessment tool, if not memorization at the end of learning? If they are inadequate, why are we still relying on these types of assessments to give us an understanding of student learning and growth?

Jo Boaler, in her book *Limitless Mind*, continues the critical look at memorization and asserts, "When we value memorization over depth of understanding, we harm the deep thinkers who turn away from the subject. We also harm the successful memorizers who would have been helped by an approach to knowledge that gave them access to deep understanding."

The Truth about Multiple-Choice Questions

For years, I gave countless multiple-choice tests and used their results to form judgments about my students' abilities. I had no other tools or training, and every teacher I knew was doing the same thing. But I always had the nagging feeling that these tests were insufficient. I knew something for sure, and you know it too: The ability to regurgitate answers on a test does not equate to true understanding. These tests told me nothing valuable about my students that I could use to better meet their needs. I had an epiphany: Multiple-choice questions do not give us rich information about student learning and growth.

To test this theory, I gave my students a literary devices test one week, and all but one of my students got an A. Yes! I must be a great teacher! Right? Not so fast. I decided to do a pop quiz using the same exact questions forty-eight hours later, and only five of those students got the A again. Five more got a B, and the rest moved down to a C with three Fs. Had I relied on that original data point, I would have thought they all understood literary devices. I did the same thing with European capitals one week later, and the results were truly devastating —but so empowering for me.

What I had always known was beginning to come to the surface. Students have to be able to apply the knowledge—and articulate this new understanding—to truly learn it. Brené Brown, the author of *Daring Greatly*, quotes a proverb that illustrates this idea perfectly:

"KNOWLEDGE IS ONLY A RUMOR UNTIL IT LIVES IN THE MUSCLE."

It is only when we use our knowledge in new and novel ways that it sticks. We have to ask ourselves: Do we accomplish this by asking kids to pick from four answer choices and bubble one in?

If you want to learn a more authentic approach to assessing student learning, you have come to the right place. We are going to look at assessments as an art form that can make you a one-of-a-kind teacher.

The Beauty of Mistakes

Our current and popular assessment methods actually teach kids to be AFRAID to make mistakes. Research is showing that this might be damaging to our students. Teachers know this—we see it in our classrooms every day. Kids stop raising their hands. Kids shut down. Kids leave classrooms dejected because education does not value mistakes.

While we can't escape multiple-choice questions in our present school systems, the point here is to understand we can collect richer forms of assessments and give students a chance to cognitively struggle to make connections. Making mistakes has to be encouraged. Besides, research has shown over and over again that students who collaborate and embrace the messy process of trial and error to get to deeper learning will actually score higher on standardized multiple-choice tests.

> For students to experience growth, they need to be working on questions that challenge them, questions that are at the edge of their understanding. And they need to be working on them in an environment that encourages mistakes and makes students aware of the benefits of mistakes. This point is critical. Not only should the work be challenging to foster mistakes; the environment must also be encouraging so that the students do not experience challenge or struggle as a deterrent. Both components need to work together to create the ideal learning experience.
>
> —**Jo Boaler**
> *Limitless Mind*

Our modern tools give us the ability to begin the shift away from traditional forms of assessment. We now have the ability to get inside every student's mind and know when they know something—and when they don't—and change instruction in real time to meet their individual needs.

How Do We Begin? Many Different Sources

To gain more powerful insight into student learning, we must start by gathering information from many different sources of assessment. Some will (and should be) less suited for a spreadsheet and more suited for the authentic and real world. This means focusing on cultivating a community of learners who are allowed to make connections with what they have learned in a variety of ways. They experiment, interact, and even play with the new information—making mistakes as they go—and explain their thinking as they progress. When students can effectively articulate their own learning journey, talk through their connections, and identify and explain patterns, the teacher and student can begin to form a learning partnership based around individual student goals.

To do this, we have to teach students to:

- Learn how to articulate their thinking—not an easy process for kids who have been told to sit quietly and listen to the teacher.

- Understand how to effectively explain these connections and patterns

Make the choice of which tools are best suited for this new endeavor and way of assessing. The right use of technology allows them to make their thinking visible.

What We Do with the Information from Formative Assessments

It is important to note here that teachers should not grade formative assessments. Students deserve the opportunity of a lower-pressure environment to fully develop, make mistakes, and learn before we grade their work.

When done properly, these assessments provide us and our students with ongoing, real-time feedback about where they are in their learning and what interventions they may need in order to achieve success. The sooner a student understands how they did on these assessments, the better. We need to make student thinking visible to the teacher and the students in this process. Formative assessments provide opportunities for students to engage in metacognitive reflection on their learning; it's during these activities that they can start thinking about their thinking, then they have agency over their learning by their own adjustments.

Chromebook apps like Flipgrid and Seesaw are perfect for this and, as a result, have become increasingly popular tools. They are cool and have flashy features which make them engaging and fun a big part of learning. They are most popular, though, because of what they can do to get at student thinking and understanding because they reveal how their brains process information. The tools' abilities to facilitate thinking help bring about transfer of knowledge.

Both Flipgrid and Seesaw allow students to simply press record and articulate their learning in words—a skill that quickly illuminates understanding in a clear, logical, and engaging way.

In fact, it's a good idea to be familiar with several great tools for your Chromebook "Assessment Tool Belt." These include:

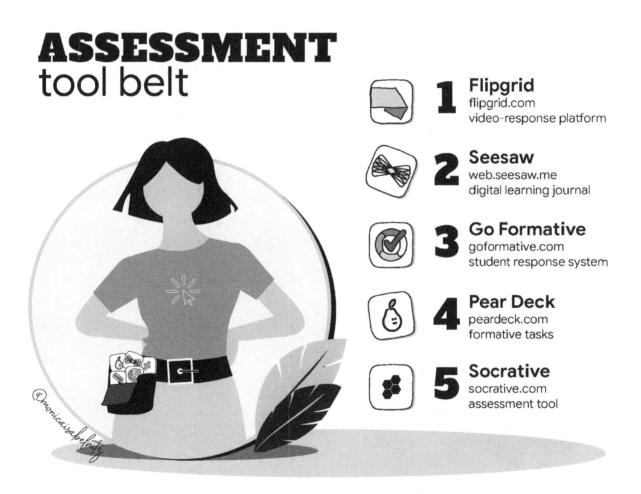

ASSESSMENT
tool belt

1 Flipgrid
flipgrid.com
video-response platform

2 Seesaw
web.seesaw.me
digital learning journal

3 Go Formative
goformative.com
student response system

4 Pear Deck
peardeck.com
formative tasks

5 Socrative
socrative.com
assessment tool

BUILDING YOUR ASSESSMENT TOOL BELT

Flipgrid (flipgrid.com)

Flipgrid is a video-response platform featuring grids and topics. Each grid is populated with topics, and the topic is where students leave their video responses or upload content. Topics empower teachers to ask different discussion questions or post prompts based on the overarching subject of the grid.

Teachers can create really quick and easy checks for understanding. Even the students who are shy, or slow to respond, or don't typically raise their hands have an opportunity to participate with Flipgrid. It works great for students who just need a bit more time to process before they post. It also allows students to build articulate verbal reasoning skills as they post and respond. Video responses often prompt further discussions among students in the class.

> Take an hour and learn how to use Flipgrid in your classroom: **infused.link/online**

TEACHERS CAN CREATE REALLY QUICK AND EASY CHECKS FOR UNDERSTANDING.

Infographic by Holly Clark @HollyClarkEDU for OnlineLearningIdeas.com.

Seesaw (web.seesaw.me)

Seesaw is a digital learning journal. It can be accessed from any device with online access, and it should be a critical and well-used learning tool for any type of assessment—especially formative assessment.

Seesaw is a very simple way for students to record and share what's happening as they progress through the learning process using the six powerful tools: photo, drawing, video, upload, notes, and adding a link.

In addition, hearing their classmates' responses enables students to fill in gaps in their own learning or discover that they might have missed some important information. They might even discover where they are excelling and get to know themselves better as learners.

↘ Check out this blog post for a tutorial and ways to do incredible assessments with Seesaw: **infused.link/checkswithseesaw**

Go Formative (goformative.com)

Formative is a powerful web-based tool that's perfect for gathering information about student learning. It offers students multiple ways to respond, including the ability to write on their screens. This then allows them to see the process they went through to solve a problem such as a math equation.

Teachers can quickly gather both text-based and graphical information about your students' learning and growth. With that information, you can better provide students with resources to assist in understanding concepts with which they may be struggling.

This tool is amazing for all teachers, but it is particularly useful for math and science.

Pear Deck (peardeck.com)

Pear Deck is a tool you add to Google Slides, through the Add-ons setting in your toolbar, that helps teachers layer on formative tasks that provide insight into how students are doing with comprehension of content and ideas.

Teachers can engage students in their learning during those times of needed direct instruction. Simply add Pear Deck to an already made Slide deck. They can add interactive elements to each slide by choosing to add text, choice, number options, push out web content and allow students to draw or have them drag content to the right place.

Using the teacher dashboard, teachers can view all of the responses and choose to keep this information private or share it out with the entire class by projecting the answers on the screen. In this way, students can learn from each other.

Students can access Pear Deck very easily. They use a code that is displayed by the teacher. Students head to joinpd.com on their devices and use the code to get started. It is very easy and super engaging for students.

Socrative (socrative.com)

Socrative is a website and app that allows you to quickly gather information about your students' learning in the form of closed and open-ended questions. There is also a game-like response area called "Space Race." For our purposes, we will discuss the Quick Question option. This option is one of the choices found on the app's Launchpad or front page: socrative.com.

It allows you to hear from every student in your class, not just the few who raise their hands to answer questions. You can use the Quick Question option to do a quick Check for Understanding that will illuminate in a short amount of time what the students have learned.

Students' answers appear on the screen, allowing them to compare their responses with their peers' as they finish. Plus, Socrative gives you access to a saved copy of your class's responses for later and saves it using Google Drive, so you can do a lot of manipulation of student data.

As students compare their answers with their classmates, they enter a state of metacognition as they think about one another's answers in comparison with their own, prompting them to continue learning even after they've responded. This tool also allows students to vote on the best answer from everyone's responses.

TRY EACH OF THESE TOOLS IN YOUR CLASSROOM TO SEE WHICH ONES WORK BEST WITH YOUR STUDENTS. YOU WILL FIND THEY WILL BE FAR SUPERIOR TO SIMPLE MEMORIZATION AND REGURGITATION FOR UNLOCKING OUR STUDENTS' POTENTIAL.

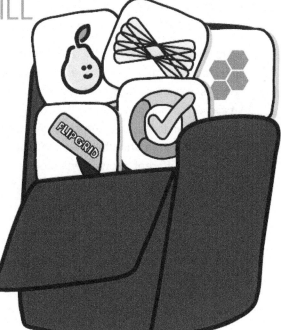

As teachers, we need to be able to understand the **process of learning** that each student goes through to solve complex problems or accomplish unique learning goals. We can do this through a process purposefully labeled: Press Record.

It is called Press Record because technology provides an easy way to enable students to record or narrate the learning as it happens. This **makes their thinking and understanding visible**. Students explain their thinking process, expound as needed on that process, and share their work by simply pressing record. This exercise is appropriate for all the steps of the learning journey. We do this so we as educators can know more about our students as individual learners.

When we allow time for this, we really step up our digital pedagogy game. This change in how we gather student data is important for both the teacher and the student. It allows learners to see growth over time—and to begin to discover individual strengths and weaknesses. And it gives teachers the ability to see students as individuals with different growth trajectories, different learning needs, and different perspectives. Armed with this understanding, we can better help guide students toward their full potential.

We can do this for:
- Checks for Understanding
- Demonstrations of Learning
- Transfer of Knowledge—applying the learning to a new and novel situation
- Reflections

Tools that are great for making thinking visible include:

- Seesaw
- Flipgrid
- Book Creator
- Screencastify
- Slides and PowerPoint
- Adobe Spark
- OneNote

Technology tools are varied, providing teachers and students alike with great options to choose from in order to suit their needs.

Language Arts

Before technology, English teachers had few options other than the one-dimensional routine of an essay, stapled, and turned in. More often than not, they made comments that students did not read, assigned a letter grade, and moved on to the next essay without much understanding of what students did and did not learn. But now, technology provides better channels to demonstrate learning. Let's say a student turning in an essay needs to illuminate the process that led to the final product. They can bring that paper on the screen and use Screencastify to talk about what they wrote, highlighting parts they are most proud of and underlining word choice for a section they took a lot of time to craft. They might also discuss the process they went through to write the paper. They submit that final screencast and its illuminating details along with the paper. The teacher, watching the screencast, gains a better understanding of the student's process and what to address for improvement. They can also give kudos in a specific way for problem-solving, great choices, clear understanding, and so much more. This feedback goes much further than a letter grade in fostering deep learning. And the student feels more comfortable with accountability and the need for critically analyzing their work as they go.

Math

In math, students can go into the real world and find examples of where a math concept is used in real life. They can tackle higher-level thinking mathematical questions and real-world applications to explore, both as individuals and collaboratively. Using a tool like Seesaw or Flipgrid, they can consider a problem, make connections, talk through more than one process, and attempt a solution. They can use Seesaw or Flipgrid to record and explain how they came to understand the problem and its connections and arrive at a solution. Once they submit their explanations and thinking process, a teacher can evaluate the process and give students better insight into their own abilities to problem-solve. They can also point out student success and insight, building confidence—and maybe even inspiring students to tackle other problems on their own.

Technology provides multidimensional learning approaches that allow students to make connections, explain different perspectives, and better understand themselves as learners. Giving students the tools to explain their learning process empowers them to better understand themselves. This is where true transformational teaching and learning begin to happen.

ASSESSMENT FOR/AS/OF LEARNING

Truly powerful assessments understand the For/As/Of Assessment framework. Here is a breakdown of Assessment For/As/Of Learning:

Assessment for Learning

An **assessment** *for* **learning**, or formative assessment, is exactly what it sounds like: It's an assessment that helps us understand where our students are in the learning process. However, in this case, we don't grade these assessments. Rather, when done properly, they provide us and each of our students with ongoing, real-time feedback about where they are in their learning and what interventions they may need to achieve success. These assessments also allow us to make just-in-time adjustments to our classroom instruction and provide students with valuable insights into which areas they may need to focus their attention.

Assessment as Learning

An **assessment** *as* **learning** is an ongoing assessment that students do to reflect on and monitor their progress. By asking students to record their reflections and processes using a tool like Screencastify, we're encouraging them to think about their learning process, make their thinking visible, and help them take responsibility for achieving their personal learning goals. By doing this type of assessment, students are more likely to ask for and receive feedback from others.

This feedback can be critical to helping them understand their own areas of strength and need.

Assessment of Learning

An **assessment** *of* **learning** is the "summative evaluation" of a student's work. In this case, we measure a student's work against the predetermined learning criteria to see if they've demonstrated an understanding of the intended learning targets. Generally, students' final creations and work give us more insight into their learning and personal growth than an assessment composed of multiple-choice questions ever could.

Consideration: Typically, summative assessments take place at the end of a unit and look at a standardized proficiency, judging individual students by everyone else's progress. Instead of asking the same questions and having a blanket target for all of our students, though, we should look for student growth on an individual scale. We should find out what each student knows at the beginning of a unit then determine individualized targets. This allows us to throw out percentages and measure our well-defined learning targets against the student-led conferences and evidence of learning we glean from their portfolios. By doing this, we grade students on their individual growth, not where we expect everyone to be.

WE GRADE STUDENTS ON THEIR INDIVIDUAL GROWTH, NOT WHERE WE EXPECT EVERYONE TO BE.

DIGITAL WRITING

Historically in education, we have not been able to observe the writing process in the same way we can today with digital tools. Going from analog to digital writing means that we expand and enrich the true process of writing. Using digital tools like Google Docs Revision History and SAS Writing Reviser (see below) provides better ways for students to clarify the writing process and pinpoint areas of growth. It is the entire process of writing that should be evaluated, not just the final product, because it serves kids much better to know HOW to assemble a narrative than WHAT to write. The experience can become much richer using a mapped-out workflow and a Chromebook.

These days, adults rarely sit down in analog to write a narrative. Most people go directly to something like a Google Doc and begin typing. Since we have not been taught how to brainstorm digitally, we often skip that step and don't teach it to our students—and we are not sure how it all works.

> Packaging a writing unit into a HyperDoc is something that would be useful for keeping students on task and helping them better understand the flow of the writing process.

A Student-Centered Writing Process

The following process will show the workflow of a more digitally fluent and process-rich writing environment.

Brainstorming

Students need to talk through what they want to say, and they can benefit from access to that original thought process as they continue to write. For this stage, consider these two learning tools:

Flipgrid (flipgrid.com)

This important brainstorming tool is often underutilized. To learn Flipgrid, you can access the FREE online course at **bit.ly/Flipgrid19**. Have students break down the task like this:

1. Make a Writing Grid–For this example, we will use Persuasive Writing.

2. Under the Grid of Persuasive Writing, make a topic called 'brainstorming' and have students talk through their ideas aloud. This will allow them to discuss their ideas first with the teacher in a low-pressure environment. You can reply to these or simply give them a chance to talk through it without your input.

3. Students can also listen and reply to each other on the grid for a more collaborative process.

Padlet (padlet.com)

This is another great **brainstorming** tool. Students can have their own Padlet account. (They get three Padlets free.) They can use the squares of a grid like they would with sticky notes, moving them around as they expand, change, and work through the process. Here they can keep notes with the arrangement of ideas and have a digital workflow with a clear visual component.

> **Analog:** Have students use paper to create mind maps to organize thoughts and chunks of information. Remember, it's always okay to go analog!

Digital Research and Digital Curation

Gathering information and keeping it for future reference is a useful skill in the digital world, but it takes time to develop. This digital curation is key, and it can be amplified by these two tools:

Google Keep (keep.google.com)

Google Keep is both a web platform and a cool Chrome extension that allows students to take very thoughtful notes, color code those notes, share them with classmates, and add labels to them by topic.

This amazing program is automatically added to the side of any Google Doc so that students can see their writing side-by-side with their notes and also take notes while constructing their draft. **This important tool should not be overlooked in its organizational significance.**

It is here that they can also make an outline of their paper's organizational structure or tasks they still need to complete. Consider sharing task lists with students that give them an idea of what is expected in the paper or to remind them of the ideas they might be focusing on, like word choice or sentence structure. They can show this task list and have it open next to their Google Doc before they begin writing.

Wakelet (wakelet.com)

Wakelet is a newer tool that allows students surfing the web for information to create collections of curated research for later use.

In these collections, students can add information they find while researching. Based on this, if students are doing research on The Twenty-One California Missions, they can name a collection "San Diego Mission de Alcala" and add information they can revisit later when they begin the writing process. They can also decide which sources they want to use and which they will discard. They can even share these with other students. This helps students curate their research in a more visually appealing way. As they create collections, they also become more digitally fluent researchers.

Students can follow easy steps for a helpful digital curation tool:

1. Install the Wakelet Chrome extension.

2. Searching for relevant information, choose ideas to revisit.

3. Click on the Chrome Extension that is now placed to the right of the address bar.

4. Add that resource to the intended collection or make a new collection right from the extension.

The Drafting Process

Composing–You are on a Chromebook, so of course, Google Docs is the tool to use here—although some students enjoy Microsoft's OneNote. Students compose a draft and share it with the teacher for meaningful feedback and encouragement using the comments feature.

> ### Important
> At any point in this process, you can quickly review student work and assess the level of understanding of revision, the comments peer editors make, and the degree to which writers accept good editorial advice. This keeps the emphasis on the PROCESS rather than the PRODUCT.

Consider using the add-on, **SAS Writing Reviser.** This Google Docs add-on helps students consider good usage and fluency in their writing through a variety of tools that give advice on everything involved with sentence structure such as dangling modifiers or passive voice. It is like having a little writing mentor right to the side of your draft! This digital assistant does not take the place of good foundational grammar and sentence structure instruction, so writers should think critically before accepting the proposed correction.

Dictation–Some students might do better by dictating their writing into Google Docs. Simply go to Tools and Voice Typing, and click on the microphone which will place itself in the left-hand margin of the doc. Tap Click to Speak to begin.

Text to Speech–It is also valuable to teach students how to use text to speech on a Chromebook so they can have the computer read the story aloud to them, thereby giving them a chance to "hear" any problems in grammar or flow. This can also be done with a Text Help extension—EVERY school should have this as part of their Chromebook rollout—AND **the text to speech option is free!**

Peer Revision on a Chromebook

Students share their document with a peer editor who can now give advice via comments or suggested edits using the SHARE icon. This is the simplest part of the process and only requires that students share the document with the intended recipient and give editing capability. This process might also involve the student sharing their Google Keep notes with the person helping them; that way, the editor can look over the notes and ideas and make comments there as well. This process continues as a typical student writing workshop where students revise, edit, and proofread until it is time for the final draft. This can even involve looking at the *Six Traits of Writing* process or Lucy Calkins for younger writers.

Final Draft

It is important that the final draft happens in another program so we can make the learning come alive the way it can't in Google Docs. Adobe Spark Page is highly recommended because it gives students a place to add important media elements to their paper that will help make their content more enjoyable to read, more colorful, and more multi-dimensional.

In Adobe Spark Page (spark.adobe.com), students first add a title and then creatively add images or even a few theme-enhancing photos using the Glideshow which creates a moving story as images glide over those photos.

This feature adds impact and visual appeal, taking the writing from the old black-and-white of 2005 and amplifying the process with images and videos that become part of the story itself. This gives simple writing the kind of digital upgrade we are looking for in a modern classroom and adds a critical thinking element as students choose graphics and images that will add value to their writing.

Go to **spark.adobe.com/edu** to have your IT enroll the district for free student and teacher accounts.

Reflection and Making Thinking Visible

Once complete, have students open up their final draft and use Screencastify (screencastify.com) to record themselves explaining what their paper is supposed to be about and why they chose the graphics they did so the teacher can understand the thinking behind their process. **This is how they make their thinking and the writing process visible to the teacher.**

This crucial step allows students to articulate their ideas and their process. **The cognitive struggle that students undergo to explain the process is one of the most important ways they can reflect and learn from what might be a one-and-done assignment.** They now have to explain in words the *why*, the *how,* and the *meaning* behind their writing choices. This is tremendously valuable for making learning permanent.

Tip: At regular intervals, have students leave videos on Flipgrid about their progress in research and writing. This way, you can better understand their thinking, find out where they are in the process, and guide them better. Offer personalized, scaffolded advice that meets students where they are in their learning. By regularly checking in, we can customize our input according to the progress and needs of each individual student.

DIGITAL RESEARCH
INFORMATION LITERACY

The Importance of Information Literacy

As more and more Chromebooks hit classrooms, many students will approach these devices the same way they approach all tech: trial, error and exploration. Kids do not typically read manuals or wait for instruction. Instead, they take an intuitive path of exploration to spontaneously find what they are looking for—usually entertainment. But in schools, students will use technology to learn, and learning opportunities come with endless information. This will be amplified considerably in the 5G era. So how can they navigate huge amounts of information in order to find what will best suit their learning needs?

Information Literacy

As we enter the 2020s with Chromebook-Infused Classrooms, information literacy is as important as foundational reading and math skills. Information literacy gives students the power to sift through massive amounts of information produced in an online search, evaluate it, and use it effectively in their learning mission. It is the key weapon in the battle against fake news.

But how can we teach a skill we have not yet mastered ourselves?

I make presentations around the globe. During one of those sessions on "Critical Thinking and the Web," I give a quick diagnostic quiz to teachers to see if they can conduct a **well-executed Google search**. Incredibly, **only five** out of nearly 5,000 participants have been able to conduct an effective search. But if educators are to keep up with the demand for information literacy, we have to acquire and teach the skill of "**Effective Searching**." If we neglect this responsibility, we create a kind of digital divide. Instead of the disparity between those who have devices and those who do not, the new divide will be between those who can evaluate information and those who cannot.

Students must know how to effectively find and curate information. Noted librarian and information specialist Helene Blowers coined the term "The New Digital Divide," and two of its facets are:

⇨ **Those who know how to "think" about search versus those who don't**

⇨ **Those who know how to validate "soft information" versus those who don't**

> While schools and districts are working to provide all students access to devices in the classroom, they must also give students the time and resources to develop critical thinking habits to spot the most accurate and relevant information. Most teachers mistakenly assume they can set students free on the internet to find information through a random search. Teachers, however, especially in the elementary and middle grades, need to develop a shared vocabulary around the skill of searching. They must ensure that their students learn some basic search strategies that are applied until critical searching skills become almost automatic.

Information literacy requires a crucial two-step teaching process:

1. Perform a well-executed Google search.
2. Validate the information their searches produce.

To help do this in your own classroom, school, or district, check out the quick guide sections on searching and validating information. This link provides an example of searching vocabulary and skills acquisition appropriate for each level in a K–12 school: **infused.link/ searching1**

A Quick Guide to Effective Searching in Your Classroom

➣ Check out this resource for more information: **infused.link/googlesearch**

1. Use Quotation Marks ""

Students should always use quotes to search for an exact word or set of words. This is useful when you want something like song lyrics or text from an exact historical time period.

Example: "The Great Chicago Fire"

This also helps make sure that Google does not give you extra, unneeded result pages that merely include one of the words in your search. For example, the Chicago Fire, a well-known soccer team, would be an included result but not necessary for the original search. Putting your search words in quotation marks helps eliminate unimportant or unhelpful results and narrows down a more targeted result.

2. Use Dashes (or the minus sign)

Use the minus symbol directly before a word to exclude it from your search results and eliminate unwanted information.

Example: "Great Chicago Fire" -soccer

3. Use Two Periods . .

Use this to specify information between two numbers or a period of time. For example, you might want to try:

"Great Chicago Fire" October 8..10

4. Site Search

Identify a specific website that narrows down the most reliable and relevant information in a search. For a look through the *Chicago Tribune* website only, do this.

site: Chicagotribune.com "The Great Chicago Fire"

5. Use Country Codes to Look Up News Stories

Students should gather every viewpoint and possible perspective on current events and historical news stories, not just those presented through the red, white, and blue-colored lenses of the US media. To do this, they can easily search using different country codes. For example, if you wanted to get to Google Korea, all you would have to do is search using the country code *Kr* for Korea.

Try it yourself first by going to Google Korea—**google.co.kr**.

Below are a few country codes, but a quick Google search of "country codes" will produce a complete list.

A List of Some of the Country Codes:

Country	Code
Australia	.au
South Korea	.kr
China	.cn
Japan	.jp
South Africa	.za
New Zealand	.nz
United Kingdom	.uk

A Validation Framework for Students—R.E.A.L.

Another critical information literacy skill is validating information found in a web search. Educator Alan November uses the acronym R.E.A.L. in his book *Web Literacy for Educators*. I began using these concepts with my students in 2008, and over a decade later it works, but it might need some updates. Here are a few steps to help students gain additional information about a website and its author. (My 2020 adaptations are in boldface.)

Read the URL

First, what does the URL tell you about the author or the source of the article? Look for words like *Smithsonian* or *New York Times* in the address. Is the website a verified information source or a private blog? What can you tell about the information you are about to examine? Read and click through all the navigation tabs to see what you can glean about the source of information, the site, and anything that will help you start thinking more critically about the content.

Examine the content

This is an essential step. The student must read the content, paying specific attention to any strong language, out-of-place wording, or elements that don't seem suited for the title.

Use **"Command F"** to search the page. With this feature, a small search bar will appear in the upper right-hand corner of the screen, and students can search for specific words or phrases. This can give students good information as to whether this is a rich information source or not.

If there are comments at the end of an article, examine them closely. Pay close attention to what they tell you about agreement or disagreement with this content. Can you get a feel for any opinions that dominate the thread? What does this tell you about the source?

Examine the images. Can you do a reverse image search to find where they came from? (Put an image into Google Search to see where it came from.) Does this tell you anything important?

Ask about the author

Try whois.com and place the address of the site into the search bar to see who owns the site. Look for the *About* section, or maybe the author is directly listed on the first page. If you can find the author, dig into their social media presence. Search their social accounts and see what the person is posting on other sites. What can we learn about this person from their other posts? **(Note: Only conduct social media searches with kids over thirteen.)**

Look at the Links (and More)

Who links to this website? To find out, use **moz.com/researchtools/ose**. Once there, add the address of the site you are validating and begin your query. This will give you some very interesting rating information about the site and list what sites link to this source. Look at those sites to see if you can critically analyze what those sites might tell you about the information you are validating.

Look at the shares. How many people shared the information? Is it popular? This might help you decide whether you want to spend time with this information or if you should consider using it as a source for your research. Popularity does not mean the article is always better, but sites that have been shared have better exposure, and fallacious arguments or facts will most likely have been called out.

Finally, use a Google Form for students to submit validated sites. They only do this after all R.E.A.L. steps have been completed and they feel they have the information they need to validate the source. This will give the teacher a place (the spreadsheet) to check student analysis and research against those sources cited in their paper.

Here is an example form: **infused.link/realform**

How "Filter Bubbles" Affect a Search

The term "filter bubbles" means the algorithms that work to steer a search toward an unintentionally biased result. The hidden power behind search results works like this:

Every online search is conducted through filters. Based on your past search history, these filters work to narrow down what results *you would most likely want*, often leaving out opposing viewpoints. So your past searches, preferences, and location will affect the search results. The scary part is that **you do not get to decide what gets filtered out.**

For this reason, it is helpful to teach students how to search in the Chrome browser's *Incognito* mode by going to File—> New Incognito Window. On some Chromebooks, you can find it on the left-hand side under the three dots. This way, you don't reveal who you are to search engines, and they can't filter your results. To learn more, watch this very informative TED Talk by author Eli Pariser. **infused.link/filterbubbles.**

The incognito window is turned off in some districts—but a great alternative is to have something like Mobile Guardian (mobileguardian.com) installed to enable students to search in incognito while allowing schools to monitor student searches for safety purposes.

If we fail to take information literacy seriously and do not work to see that it is implemented across the curriculum, student ability to conduct an objective search is compromised. A world driven by algorithms and 'likes' takes power away from individuals and their ability to be truly informed.

Consider taking the lead at your school to make sure all students are literate and fluent in information acquisition, effective search, and validating content. The world might just be a better place if you do!

Please consider watching *The Great Hack* on Netflix, if you can, or this TEDx Talk—**infused.link/facebookbrexit**

VALIDATING INFORMATION IS ONE OF THE MOST IMPORTANT SKILLS WE MUST TEACH IN THE 2020s. THIS YEAR, MAKE IT A GOAL TO HELP STUDENTS BECOME MORE INFORMATION LITERATE. THEY WILL THANK YOU FOR IT!

DIGITAL READING:
A LOVE OF READING

Reading has always been a layered and complex task. Beginning with letter and word recognition, it should progress to comprehension, visualization, critical thinking, and deep questioning. The goal for most educators, if you are like me, is to pass along a love for words and the thrill of a good story, with timeless themes that illustrate the human condition, characters, and places that leave indelible impressions. You want your students to connect with that story on a heart level and know the joy of getting lost in a great book.

More than ever, we also want our students to effectively manage the huge amount of information available to them, read and evaluate it critically, distinguish fact from opinion, and use reading to make informed choices.

Every school subject involves reading. For their future success, all of our students need to be fluent readers. Unfortunately, many students view reading as an unpleasant task or a chore—a necessary evil instead of a joy—because sometime in their educational experience, they hit a roadblock. They had difficulty progressing. Possibly even worse, they lost interest in material that was not relevant to them. This should be a cause for alarm.

Skimming Is Not Reading

Today, most people's reading has little depth. It consists of scrolling through social media or headlines at checkout stands. The advent of technology means digital reading is the primary way to gather information, so many people now simply skim online content, encounter some sensational 'clickbait' headlines, and repeat the headlines to their friends as if they read the entire article. Worse yet, without critical thinking or analysis, they pass a single statement along on social media platforms—often propagating misinformation (fake news) without even knowing it.

We can't blame our students for this trend and say their smartphones make them lazy—everyone is susceptible to being misinformed. That is why learning how to read digitally has become an increasingly important skill.

Technology has dramatically multiplied the amount of information available to us. Today, we approach text differently than we did in the past, and we have to teach our students crucial skills. This section will take a look at how we can help students use technology to find meaning and context in their reading books and in their digital reading of text. Whether students are reading digitally or on paper, *The Chromebook Infused Classroom* has great tools to enhance the process.

How Collaboration Helps

We used to think of reading as a solitary task, but today collaboration is indispensable for both struggling students and those who are more advanced with the cognitive process of reading. In her book, *Limitless Mind,* Jo Boaler says,

> "WHAT IS IMPORTANT IS TO DEEPLY UNDERSTAND THINGS AND THEIR RELATIONS TO EACH OTHER."

To do this, we have to give students the space to talk about their reading and work collaboratively through the issues being presented in text. A reading partnership provides a great place to connect and see patterns that we need to understand—the pieces that form the whole.

When learners collaborate, they have to make sense of another person's opinion, think about how that works, and put it with the schema of their own thinking. They learn to respectfully wrestle through any differences in perspectives and try to get to the truth. With collaborative efforts, students must learn to work with other people and find ways to exist together in spite of initial discomfort. Collaboration in the cognitive struggle of reading is a real-world skill that benefits our students and fuels learning as they grapple with text and meaning. Students will use this skill long after they have left your classroom—wouldn't it be great if they loved collaboration AND reading?

To help students learn that reading can be both a really exciting activity and that it does not always have to happen alone, we can use technology to make reading both collaborative and fun!

Here are some tools that can help you make that happen.

Your Tool Belt for Enhancing the Digital Reading Experience with Collaboration—Use the Ones That Work for Your Classroom

Google Docs Commenting and Highlighting

When you want to go paperless or just have a place for students to interact with digital reading, Google Docs makes a great first step. Teachers can find short stories and other reading content and bring it into Google Docs. By doing this, students can work closely with the text and even begin to collaboratively comment and work through text with other students. This type of collaborative reading will be an important skill in their future education and in life.

With Google Docs, students can do the following:

- Use commenting to interact with text and another student.
- Use commenting to keep notes as they read.
- Use the highlighter in the toolbar to highlight important sections and ideas for later discussions.
- Use the Writers Highlighter Add-on to keep track of highlights and color coding in a side-bar.
- Take important ideas or quotes and add to Google Keep to use later as evidence or comparisons.
- Collaboratively comment on a reading with another student **or share with the entire class.**
- Use comments to identify and elaborate a literary device used by the author.
- Use the Chrome Extension Talk and Comment to leave voice notes **as a place to make student thinking and learning visible.**

All of the above can be shared with the teacher and **allow for student voice.**

Text Help for Education—Read&Write Chrome Extension.
Universal Design for Learning Tool

Text Help is truly one of the best tools out there for readers. It is a tool bar that attaches itself to a Google Doc or website.

⇨ Teachers get this tool for free—head to **infused.link/texthelp**

- *Student accounts must be purchased by the school or district.*
- This is an *Infused Classroom top tool,* and this extension should be on a Chromebook device!

What Read&Write for Google Chrome Extension does:

- Text to speech can read information to students.
- Use the highlighter to highlight important ideas.
- Even download an MP3 of the reading from a Google Doc or website, for on-the-go listening using the AudioMaker feature. Think of how this could help the struggling reader.
- Use the picture dictionary to help students with text and comprehension.

- Vocabulary List tool can help kids keep track of vocabulary by auto-populating it into a Google Doc.

- Using the Practice Reading Aloud Tool allows students to record themselves reading and send that to their teacher as a reading fluency test.

- Add Voice notes to a doc or reading activity.

Book Creator

Book Creator is a Chrome-based app that you can find at **app.bookcreator.com**

This is an *Infused Classroom Top Tool* and should be used in every reading and writing classroom.

All students and teachers need is a Google account to get started. This app allows students to create books—or in this case, to keep track of their reading by taking interactive notes and adding these to a learning journal of their reading unit. Below is a link to an example unit done with the book *Wonder* with a middle-grade classroom.

> Example: Book *Wonder* and Reading Journal, **infused.link/wonder**

With Book Creator, students can:

- Illustrate a book that is not already illustrated to demonstrate they comprehend the theme and story plot. These books can be **shared with the class in the library.**

- Take a picture of the book—bring that into Book Creator and record themselves reading that page to capture fluency.

- Bring in graphics like maps to show a location and geographic movements of a book—then **use the record feature to explain why** these are important to the plot of the book.

- Make picture dictionaries or vocabulary journals.

- Create acrostic poems of characters' names and then use the record button to **explain their thinking,** commenting on why they chose the words and ideas they did.

- Keep a character journal or diary and then record a video as that person **explains their perspective** at the end.

- Work collaboratively in a book to compare and contrast, predict, or reflect on a story. **This way they can share their work with one another.**

- Create a quote short story. They gather quotes during the reading of a book that, when pieced together and read, summarize the story effectively. Students use the **record feature to explain their selections.**

- Add explanations or videos that help them understand parts of the book that might be unfamiliar. For example, where is Tulsa on a map of the US, and what does the city look like? (Teachers can do this too!)

Seesaw (web.seesaw.me)

Seesaw is a learning journal where kids respond to activities or tasks set by the teacher. These responses live in the class journal and allow students to see one another's work and learn from one another. They give the student a chance to both work alone or collaboratively and then **share their work with the class.**

This is an *Infused Classroom top tool*, and this app should be used in every reading and writing classroom.

Students can:

- Interact with text by taking certain text and drawing or adding a visual that represents the selection, then **explain their thinking** using the record feature.

- Create plot maps and then use the record feature to **explain the plot in greater detail.**

- Respond to a reading passage by selecting the most impactful words and then **explaining their choices** using the record feature.

Teachers can:

- Create folders of book genres and **all students can add their voice** by adding their favorite books, with video reviews, in the corresponding folder.

- Teachers can create reading fluency journals **for each student to record reading fluency** over time.

- Teachers can create phonics-based activities to help students learn to sound out words. See the Activity Library.

- Send home a passage, story theme, or type of genre you want parents to read from at home.

Insert Learning

Insert Learning is a Chrome Extension that allows teachers to create interactive online reading assignments for students. Simply install the extension, choose an online reading, select the extension, and a toolbar will be placed in the left-hand side of the screen.

Teachers can:

- Add interactive discussion questions of varying types.

- Embed additional content like videos, Flipgrid, Edpuzzles and Quizlets—anything that has an embed code.

- Monitor student responses in real time.

- Insert sticky notes on the webpage.

- Assign a reading to a class.

- Add close-reading questions.

- Pair this with reading content like **Newsela.com**—an amazing resource for current reading content.

Students can:

- Interact with the reading the teacher has populated with questions or resources.

- Annotate web pages by pen; highlighting and sticky notes and the annotations stay with the reading piece when they return.

- Learn how to better interact with online text.

Wakelet

Wakelet is a curation tool, much like Pinterest but a tad more student and education-friendly. It's so easy and such a powerful tool for students to organize ideas around reading.

Students can:

- Curate all kinds of resources into Wakelet Collections—much like Pinterest boards—by including photos, links, videos, social media posts, PDFs, Flipgrid videos, and items from their Google Drive. Students can do this directly in wakelet.com or add the Chrome Extension and simply click on it to add something directly from the web.

- Keep collections of their favorite books. They can edit the information card to include their own book review, adding stars or emojis to the review.

Teachers can:

- Create Wakelet collections to add important background knowledge or activate curiosity by gathering additional reading resources, like videos and web content, to help bring reading assignments to life.

For more information, see the Wakelet section at the back of the book.

Edji.it

Developed by an elementary teacher for his own class, this is an interactive reading tool that allows kids to highlight, comment, and get really involved in the reading—individually or as a group. To learn more about what students and teachers can do with this tool, check out all the cool things it can do in the back of the book.

OneNote

While OneNote is a Microsoft Tool, omitting it here would not be fair to students who would flourish by using this organizational and interactive tool. OneNote is a digital and interactive binder extraordinaire, allowing for collaboration, making connections with text, analyzing patterns, and storing information for later use.

By signing in with their Google accounts, students can:

- Interact with text by annotating, recording fluency, and working collaboratively with the teacher or other students.

- Use Immersive Reader to read text to students, translate, and utilize the picture dictionary and colored screens to eliminate reading fatigue.

- Share with the teacher all reading notes and reading fluency audio.

- Take collaborative sketchnotes as they engage with a reading.

- Get immediate feedback on annotations from the teacher.

Video link **infused.link/onenote1**

DIGITAL MATH

Teaching math digitally can require some rethinking of traditional methods. It means learning to let students begin the process of uncovering the beauty of math in everyday life on their own, outside of the traditional direct instruction model. I once worked with a teacher who used the Harkness Method. On Monday, the teacher gave students some really hard math problems (that could not be Googled) and allowed students to work collaboratively to solve them without his direct instruction, though he was available to offer guidance. The kids wrestled with the problems all week, writing their ideas all over the whiteboard walls. It was a thing of beauty to observe them working together to solve rich and complex problems. On Friday, the teacher listened to solutions and offered input. I used to walk by that classroom envious I had not been taught math in that way.

Once they got used to it, the students really seemed to love this method. They adapted easily to this new form of self-directed discovery that leads to rich understanding.

This type of teaching requires a shift from the drills and memorization of rote learning to authentic understandings. It's not easy to do when you feel the pressure of standards and high-stakes tests. One person leading the way toward more authentic learning, though, is Jo Boaler, and her book *Mathematical Mindsets* should sit at every math teacher's bedside.

↘ Check out the book here: **infused.link/mathmindset**

As a start, Boaler writes about the importance of explaining how students arrived at an answer, even if the answer they got was correct. She writes, "Explaining your work is what, in mathematics, we call *reasoning*, and reasoning is central to the discipline of mathematics."

Enter Flipgrid and Seesaw. Both platforms allow teachers to create amazing opportunities for students to articulate their thinking and explain their ideas and understanding. It also allows us to identify where they might have gaps in their learning. Both platforms enable teachers to respond to students quickly and easily because the responses are easily recorded and viewed. We can differentiate instruction when we know where kids have excelled or might be having problems uncovering concepts.

For example, is your class doing word problems? Have students show how they solved the problem using the whiteboard in Seesaw or Flipgrid and then record over it while explaining their steps to find the solution. They can then view their classmates' responses and even self-correct as they watch others explain their thinking. This enables students to critically think about their ideas in comparison with others', otherwise known as *metacognition*. This is an important strategy in the true understanding of math concepts.

 Tip: The new shorts camera in Flipgrid and the new pen tools in Seesaw allow kids to do their math problems on a white board while explaining the process

Inquiry in Mathematics

Jo Boaler also expands the practice of teaching to include the idea of exploration in our learning about math. She points out: "Include inquiry opportunities. Ask the problem *before* teaching the method. Add a visual component and ask students how they *see* the mathematics. Extend the task to make it lower floor and higher ceiling. Ask students to convince and reason; be skeptical."

> Use Flipgrid or Seesaw to make math visible in your classroom.

The good news is that Chromebooks are so good at helping teachers accomplish this! The Chromebook has some magical features for creating real-word examples and letting students grapple with and construct knowledge around math concepts.

Most teachers know about the online tools, Desmos and Equatio, designed to make math learning truly authentic by empowering kids to discover their love of math and numbers.

Desmos, a free online graphing calculator, helps students see how math is used in many real-world circumstances and includes pre-populated activities that are easy to use. It includes coaching help and a dashboard that allows teachers to see what students are doing as they are working through the problems.

The Chrome Extension Equatio takes the pain out of creating equations and graphs digitally and allows teachers to easily make practice questions for students. They can even dictate a math equation into the program, and it will produce a corresponding digital problem. You have to see this for yourself! Check it out here: **infused.link/ equatio**

OneNote also does this equation creation seamlessly. It might be something worth investigating to help math students do their math homework and keep track of their learning in an infinite canvas—a skill talked about in the Infused Classroom Student.

Any math teacher wanting to change instruction to allow for more use of the Chromebook should start by looking up these four experts to discover how technology can be harnessed to improve teaching and learning in math:

- Jo Boaler, *Mathematical Mindsets*—**infused.link/mathmindset**
- John Stevens, *Table Talk Math* and *The Classroom Chef: Sharpen Your Lessons, Season Your Classes, Make Math Meaningful*—**infused.link/ tabletalkmath**
- Alice Keeler, *Teaching Math with Google Apps: 50 G Suite Activities*—**infused.link/googlemath**
- Kyle Pearce and Jon Orr, *Making Math Moments that Matter*—**makemath-moments.com**

Don't be afraid to start simple by just having students use Flipgrid to explain their thinking. To learn more, there is a free online class to get started with Flipgrid: **infused.link/online**

Integrating Geo Tools into the Curriculum and Chromebooks

Special Spotlight: Jeffery Heil (@jheil65)

One of the most amazing web-based tools for the Chromebook is Google **Geo Tools**. Most of our curriculum features a geographical or "real world" aspect, and we want our students to understand all the elements that inform their view of themselves and the perspectives of others. Geo Tools infused curriculum has rich, varied, and engaging information that creates a true global awareness. Free of cost, educators can use Chromebooks to tap into these geography-based tools, widening frontiers and changing the way students interact with the curriculum and the world.

Google Earth

What it is: Google Earth is a web-based program that works on any Chromebook or Chrome browser. It allows students to explore the world from several vantage points. Students can explore 3-D cities, taking guided tours with a feature called **Voyager**. They can measure distance and area anywhere on the globe—all without leaving the classroom. Google calls the application "The World's Most Detailed Globe." Once students dive in and explore, they will find a true window on the world.

Currently, there are so many access points into the program. To activate curiosity, allow students to search places and obtain information from knowledge cards before a unit. They become virtual explorers, winding their way through cities rendered in 3-D. Using the Voyager feature, they can discover the unique story that every place on the earth has to tell. Teachers can take any place, any bookmark, or even content from Voyager and send it directly to their own Google Classroom to create discussions, assignments, or announcements tailored especially to their own students.

For a video explanation: **infused.link/geotools.**

Google Earth is also constantly updating information in real time, plus or minus fifteen minutes, so students learn and explore virtually as if they were actually in the most faraway and remote locations. For example, in an earth science class, students can access the **layers** tab in Voyager to explore sea floor depth, water surface temperature, current global weather and temperature, precipitation, and global wind speed. They can do the same thing the following day, collecting different information. After that, they can draw their own conclusions about climate trends and other environmental factors. Rather than simply learning *about* exploration, they are actually *doing* it.

How it can be used: In many learning environments and multiple ways, students can work alone or collaborate to study the landscapes that affect our climate and Gross Domestic Product (GDP) and even construct knowledge around the five themes of geography. Using relevant and engaging data, learners can even juxtapose how a geographer, a historian, and a scientist might see the same landscape differently.

No longer are we looking at a one-dimensional map in a textbook. Now we can virtually go anywhere in the world. Students in large American cities can watch firsthand the precipitation of sub-Saharan Africa in real time, climb Machu Pic-

chu, visit mud huts in Africa and skyscrapers in Dubai, and learn about the lives of people in new and exciting landscapes. The classroom becomes a gateway to inspiration and discovery.

Google Earth Education has great educational resources such as activities and lessons on various subjects. Updated information can be used and revised according to students' paths of discovery in time for class the next day. Simply go to Google Earth, open Voyager, tap on the education tab, and scroll to find relevant content.

⇨ To get started, go to **earth.google.com**

Google Tour Creator

What it is: Google Tour Creator uses VR technology, allowing you and your students to create personalized, immersive 360° tours right from your Chromebook. For a few years now, teachers have been creating experiences using **Google Expeditions**, an app that allows a teacher to guide students through pre-created augmented reality (AR) and VR lessons. It also has a very cool self-guided tour option.

Now with Google Tour Creator, teachers can customize student experiences and create their own 360° content by adding 360° imagery they create, or use from **Google Street View**, and also add photographs into the tour as points of interest.

How it can be used: If you want your students to become more creator than consumer, you can have them create their own narrated tour of a location in 360° by using Google Tour Creator. This tour can incorporate your own 360° or 180° photos and any image from Google Street View. For example, if you were studying the Greek Empire, you or your students could create tours from content accessible directly through Tour Creator. This includes adding photo-enhanced points of interest, background music, and narration from the students themselves.

⇨ Visit **infused.link/tourcreator** to see a student example from a fourth grader doing a state report. Make sure to play her narration as she talks you through the great state of California.

Teachers can add tours to their own Expedition library and facilitate students' own tours through Google Expeditions. We can leverage the power of Expeditions to showcase student-created work in a whole class environment or in a station rotation. With reflection activities, students can hypothesize and write about what they saw and experienced and ask relevant, cross-curricular questions that increase the connection between students and their world. Students need VR sets for this, which you can request funding for from organizations like Donors Choose (donorschoose.org).

To get started, go to **poly.google.com/creator/tours**

Google Arts and Culture

What it is: **Google Arts and Culture (GAC)** is one of the newest—and coolest—Google Tools. Extremely high-resolution images of artwork from almost every museum in the world can be viewed in 360° on a Chromebook or viewed in full VR through a VR viewer. Arts and Culture has searchable artifacts and collections from famous time periods and people throughout history. From primary source photography to the study of artists or historical figures, GAC can be integrated into any subject area. It is the perfect companion to allow students to visually tell a story in unique and interesting ways.

Features

- Access to huge collections of images from various historical periods that can be shared directly to Google Classroom

- Images of the world's art collections: paintings, sculptures, photographs, and artifact collections

- Accompanying narratives and fascinating stories

- Themed stories that deepen student understanding of what it means to live in a multicultural world

- A Google Arts and Culture **app** that allows students to tour museums in full VR using only a smartphone

- Suggestions for interesting points of art and culture nearby—students can discover treasures in their own regions

How It Can Be Used: Use Arts and Culture to research artists, mediums, art movements, historical events, historical figures, and places. A simple search of "Germany" turns up over 140,000 images, 113 collections, multiple stories, and 360° access to many places throughout the country and its history. All of this can be shared to Google Classroom. The visual nature of research and content consumption through Google Arts and Culture piques student curiosity, bringing any subject to life. A robust news feature also enables exploration of current cultural events to jump-start class discussion. Combined with other tools like Voyager, images can also be used to tell memorable visual stories.

Students can also research artifacts and imagery of ancient civilizations, gain a more meaningful visual perspective, and draw conclusions about the time period. You can even combine artifacts and curated stories to recreate an extinct culture!

Arts and Culture is the perfect knowledge construction tool, making explorers of our students.

> Lesson Ideas (from a sixth-grade social studies/ELA HyperDoc, incorporating the tools discussed here.
>
> **infused.link/geolesson**

Why Sketchnote?

Retain Information

Increase Focus

Creative Thinking

Calming activity

Multi-sensory

Helps to see the "bigger picture"

Make connections in learning

@sylviaduckworth

To get started, go to **Artsandculture.google.com**

If you have Chromebooks (or any device) in the classroom, you can now change the note-taking process to make it more modern and purposeful. Notes no longer need to be linear and text-heavy. They can now be interactive and visual!

Moving notes from analog to digital provides students an opportunity to take notes in a more meaningful and effective way through a customizable process called **Sketchnoting**. In her book, *How to Sketchnote, A Step-by-Step Manual for Teachers and Students*, Sylva Duckworth explains, "Sketchnoting is a form of visual note-taking, where you draw or doodle your thoughts, observations, or notes **in combination** with words or text. Sketchnoting is not art. It is a very personal way to document your thought process."

With Sketchnoting, sketching and drawing combine words and images to interact with information as students critically think about learning. As cognitive learning theory tells us, this experience provides students a better chance of actually remembering key ideas and information because they undergo the "cognitive struggle" they need to deepen understanding. The struggle comes from trying to match up the icons with learning and to arrange these in a way that will make sense later on as the students review their creations.

In addition to this cognitive importance, we know that visuals are much more powerful than text for learning and memory. In fact, research shows that visuals are processed 60,000 times faster than text! People remember 10 percent of what they hear, 20 percent of what they read, and 80 percent of what they **see** and do! (Source: *Images vs. Text*)

In her TEDx Talk, "Doodlers Unite!" (**infused.link/doodlers**), Sunni Brown debunks the myth that doodling is without merit in learning. She emphasizes the importance of doodling, calling it...

"AN INCREDIBLY POWERFUL TOOL . . . THAT WE NEED TO REMEMBER AND TO RE-LEARN."

Sunni goes on to say that "Doodling is really to make spontaneous marks to help yourself think. That is why millions of people doodle [and those] people who doodle when they're exposed to verbal information retain more of that information than their non-doodling counterparts. We think doodling is something you do when you lose focus, but in reality, it is a preemptive measure to *stop* you from losing focus. Additionally, it has a profound effect on creative problem-solving and deep information processing." This is because students have to critically think about the icons that will represent the information. This process has great implications on learning because of the cognitive struggle involved.

For more information, check out this article in *The Wall Street Journal*: **infused.link/doodlepower**

So why should students in Chromebook classrooms be sketchnoting? To personalize learning and promote a progression of thinking and learning toward the ultimate goal of deep understanding.

We cannot teach you *how* to Sketchnote in this book, but here are two amazing resources to help:

- **A Day of Sketchnoting Google Classroom Resource**. Use your personal Gmail account and go into classroom.google.com. Use this **code (w4zefz3)** to access the resources and videos that help students learn how to get started.

- Wakelet Collection on Sketchnoting: **inflused.link/sketchnoting**

- Sylvia Duckworth's book, *How to Sketchnote: A Step-by-Step Manual for Teachers and Students*: **infused.link/sketchnotingbook**

When You Begin to Sketchnote

Don't miss this step! Even if you don't have touchscreens, students can draw and sketch their notes on paper, take pictures of their creations, and upload those to Seesaw. In Seesaw, they can use the record feature to explain the thinking behind their notes, making their learning and understanding visible to the teacher and themselves.

Apps to Use on The Chromebook:

Autodesk Sketchbook

Auto Draw in Drawings

Book Creator (app.bookcreator.com)

Jamboard for individual and collaborative sketchnotes (jamboard.google.com)

DIGITAL BLENDED LEARNING LESSONS WITH HYPERDOCS

HyperDocs are a vital part of any Chromebook Infused Classroom. They are student-facing digital lessons that allow the teacher to create blended learning lessons that incorporate the 4Cs in every aspect of the learning cycle.

In simple terms, a HyperDoc is a lesson that a teacher designs within Google Docs or Google Slides with links to learning opportunities. HyperDocs are packaged in a way that is organized and visual, collaborative and alive, activating student curiosity.

A HyperDoc allows the teacher to become the "guide on the side" in the classroom. It provides enough structure to give students the flexibility to work at their own pace and develop the digital skills needed to be successful in the modern world. It also helps students develop the organizational skills they need to understand themselves better as learners. If done correctly, these well-planned lessons are the gold standard of digital learning.

Lisa Highfill, one of the creators of HyperDocs explains, "What makes HyperDocs unique is the delivery. Whether it be 'on tech' or 'off-tech,' these blended learning lessons can be designed to meet the needs of each teacher's classroom. Some may choose to design them for independent, self-paced learning, while others design them to blend with different instructional strategies, varying from 1:1 conferring and small group instruction to whole group teacher-directed instruction."

> Definition: A **HyperDoc** is an interactive Google Doc that changes the worksheet-and-lecture method of delivering instruction.

It is important to note that a HyperDoc is more than a digital worksheet because it is meant to be collaborative and allow students the opportunity to create, think critically, and communicate their ideas and understandings. The creation of a HyperDoc requires teachers to think through the lesson, anticipate outcomes they hope to achieve, and design with these goals in mind. The HyperDoc makes the teacher a learning designer.

What Is Great about Blended Learning HyperDocs

They are created to meet the needs of all learners. As Kelly Hilton, one of the Hyper-Docs creators writes, "HyperDoc creators ask themselves:

- Who are my students?
- What is their background knowledge?
- What do they already know, and what do I want them to know?
- What is my educational setting?

By personalizing the HyperDoc for the individual learners in your classroom, all students have universal access to learning."

Because of their rich lesson design, the shift in the delivery model of instruction, and the ability to meet the needs of all learners, a HyperDoc is an extremely important part of a Chromebook Infused Classroom!

To find help and get inspiration, use the HyperDocs Teacher Academy at **HyperDocs.co** to find examples, get help, and pull ideas from HyperDocs already created by other teachers.

> Consult *The HyperDoc Handbook* to learn how to make one then jump into The HyperDocs Facebook Community for more support at **facebook.com/groups/hyperdocs**

Multimedia Text Set

Often people who are attempting to make a HyperDoc confuse it with what is called a **Multimedia Text Set** (MMTS), so it's worth defining Hyper-Doc, an MMTS, and the very important differences between them.

A Multimedia Text Set has links to resources.

It comes in the form of a text (doc, slides, and site) with links to different media forms that have been curated with hyperlinks to help support an idea, unit of study, informational topic, or theme. Built for students to consume information, they are very powerful for students who need to explore something to activate curiosity. An MMTS can help build background knowledge while giving students the freedom to explore at their own pace and in their own way. It can also provide additional resources when needed.

This Generation Z MMTS is meant to be a curiosity activator for why we need to change instruction for teachers as we begin a day of professional development.

The Lesson Scenario: Distribute this Google Doc via Classroom or a shortened link and give students eight to ten minutes to explore the links in any way they prefer. Since this particular document is heavy in videos, ask students to work in groups and discuss their findings aloud so that you, as the guide on the side, can walk around and hear where they are in the discovery process. This is where the teacher could be asking questions or making meaningful comments that serve as deeper thinking prompts.

Here is an example: **infused.link/genz**

For further clarification, the authors of *The HyperDocs Handbook* put this chart together to help teachers understand the difference between an MMTS and a Hyper-Doc.

For teachers making the leap into using MMTS or HyperDocs in their classrooms, the easiest way to think of these tools is that they are made to help **organize** and **personalize** instruction. They are not a form of pedagogy or content.

Whether it's an MMTS or HyperDoc, both are meant to help use the technology in our classrooms to create more pedagogically sound and learner-forward experiences for our students. They are a great way for teachers to make the shift from worksheets to more meaningful learning experiences.

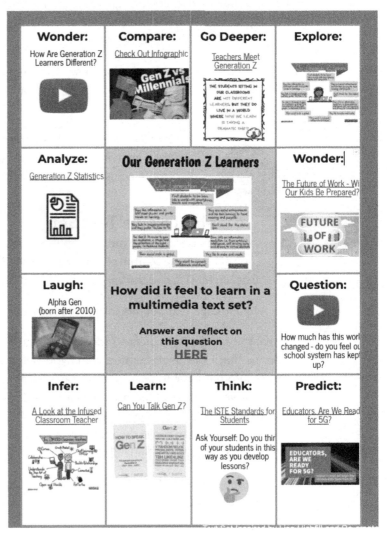

To learn more, check out these resources:

➭ HyperDoc Website: **hyperdocs.co**

➭ *The HyperDoc Handbook*: **infused.link/hyperdocs**

➭ HyperDoc Facebook Group: **facebook.com/groups/hyperdocs**

Text Sets → HyperDocs

Multimedia Text Sets...	HyperDocs...
Are a doc with links to a variety of media on a given topic for students to consume information.	Are a **digital lesson** with links to a variety of media on a given topic for students to consume information **and include one or more opportunities for students to connect beyond the classroom, collaborate, create (or show what they know), share, reflect, and/or incorporate extension activities.**
Provide opportunities for exploration of a topic.	Provide opportunities for exploration of a topic **and include multiple parts of a lesson plan all packaged in one place. Activities are self-paced or delivered in a flexible blended learning environment, differentiated with extensions and benefits of flipped classrooms to meet the needs of all students, and equip educational communities with distance learning for building inclusion.**
Build background knowledge and help with comprehension during lessons on the topic.	Build background knowledge and help with comprehension during lessons on the topic. **Package pre-teaching, teaching, and extensions for scaffolding lessons.**
Inquiry-based, offer choice, differentiated,	Inquiry-based, offer choice, differentiated, - **include accountability for formative assessment. Creators deliberately choose web tools to give students opportunities to Engage • Explore • Explain • Apply • Share • Reflect • Extend the learning**
A place to offload your lecture	A place to offload your lecture **and reimagine various ways to redefine the student learning experience. (referring to the R in the** SAMR **model)**
A chance to move around and confer with students -- more face time!	A chance to move around and confer with students -- more face time! **Teacher and peers provide immediate feedback and personalize instruction seamlessly.**

Source: The HyperDoc.co website with permission of the authors.

Remember: A HyperDoc goes more deeply into lesson design. It goes beyond consumption to include deeper thinking and learning experiences and the purposeful integration of the 4Cs into the lesson itself. With HyperDocs, it's all about the lesson design!

DIGITAL QUESTIONING:
STARTING YOUR INQUIRY JOURNEY

Apps Used to Amplify: Google Docs and Socrative

Our current education system is so obsessed with students getting the right answers. The coming years, however, will require them to ask the right questions. An effective way to start changing the delivery model of instruction is to redirect it so that **students, rather than teachers,** ask the questions. This is important because our students will live in a world where AI will have millions of answers, so asking really purposeful and well thought-out questions will be a critical skill. This shift in teaching students to ask questions instead of requiring preconceived answers can revolutionize a modern classroom.

Empowering students to ask the important questions that drive their own learning is an essential component of activating curiosity and setting their own learning goals. A great way to do this is **The Question Formulation Technique (QFT)** developed by two amazing educators, Dan Rothstein and Luz Santana.

The QFT is a six-step process in which the teacher only has ownership over one step—the first one. The rest of the process is in the hands of the students:

THE QUESTION FORMULATION TECHNIQUE

1. Design a Question Focus
2. Produce Questions
3. Work with Open-ended and Close ended questions
4. Prioritize Questions
5. Plan Next Steps
6. Reflect

Credit: Dan Rothstien and Luz Santana

As Rothstein and Santana demonstrate in their book, *Make Just One Change,* this change shifts the responsibility of question-asking from the teacher to the students. The teacher is responsible for the first step of the QFT; after that students take ownership of the rest.

To better understand this process, here is how the QFT breaks down:

Step One:

The teacher decides on the question focus that will drive this activity. For example, a teacher might have to teach about the Renaissance, so he or she would create a question focus related to this time period to stimulate student-generated questions. Students work together in groups to ask questions about this idea, theme or content.

To design a good Question Focus, the teacher applies the following rules:

➪ It has a clear focus.

➪ It is not a question.

➪ It provokes and stimulates new lines of thinking.

➪ It does not reveal teacher preference or bias.

The question focus can be a statement, a word, an image, or anything that will get students curious and asking questions.

The design of a good question focus is not easy at first, but you can consult the rightquestion.org for help and guidance.

Step Two:

Once a question focus has been formulated, write or project the Question Focus Statement, then the students must do the work of wondering by asking as many questions as they can in a limited time.

For example: The students have a time limit (I give them five minutes and use a timer.) to ask as many questions as they can about the Question Focus. For this part of the activity, I do the following tech integrations to enrich the learning.

NOTE: In this case, students use technology to amplify an important and pedagogically sound learning activity.

- Students work together in **groups of three** on the same Google Doc to ask the questions. Here is a sample: **bit.ly/QFT19**
- One student serves as the "digital scribe," typing the questions that group members collaboratively ask, while the other two watch the questions as they appear on the shared doc. This step of working on one Google Doc is very important.
- After five minutes, the groups stop and move on to the next step.

Step Three:

The next step asks the students to pick five to seven questions and change them from open-ended to closed and vice-versa. To do this:

- Teachers do need to give instruction on the difference between the two types of questions.
- The students decide if the questions they came up with are open or closed.
- If the questions are open questions, they change them to closed, and if they are closed, they change them to open.
- Students continue changing the questions for five minutes more.

This process helps students dig into the true meaning and direction of a question. This step, though hard for students, is an important exercise in critically thinking about what they are actually asking. Here is where they gain a better understanding of what makes a good question and that good questions do not always have to be open.

Step Four:

For this step, students go back to the shared doc. But now they work on their own to choose their three favorite questions. They can do this by putting their initials in the last column. The students do this step alone so that they can see what questions resonate with them, not the collective group. This process usually takes about two minutes.

During this process, however, students will be able to see those questions their group members are choosing. This visibility forces them to think deeply about their own selections, as they might begin to ask themselves why others are selecting different questions.

So that the entire class can see questions from other groups, a teacher could next use Socrative.com and the Quick Question → Short Answer option to help students see how their classmates responded.

- First, students add their favorite questions to the answer box.
- These answers are projected.
- Once all responses are in, the teacher selects Start Vote.
- With all the questions projected on each student's Chromebook screen, ask students to vote on a question they like that is different from their own.

The process of seeing other responses sends students into a state of metacognition as they compare all the different responses with what their own group generated.

Steps Five and Six:

The next steps depend on the learning goals of the class or unit. Students could now go into a research project, start a longer-term project or multimedia project, or just begin the work of learning. This step depends on the learning goals of the project. The point here is that students **activate their curiosity** before jumping into an idea, content, or unit. This is where the craft of teaching comes in. The teacher must remain a "guide on the side" and provide some scaffold direction on the final product or next steps in learning.

Finally, students will reflect on the process, which includes the entire learning journey and what they might have done differently or are most proud of.

Please make sure to check out the book these ideas came from: *Make Just One Change* by Dan Rothstein and Luz Santana.

DIGITAL WORKFLOWS WITH GOOGLE CLASSROOM

The Genius of Google Classroom

After COVID-19 we are all probably familiar with Google Classroom, but there are some really effective ways to use this tool and we will look closer at that here.

A powerful learning hub, Google Classroom is pure genius for keeping everyone in class organized and up-to-date. Here is a quick overview of its best feature. The section ends with a few nuggets to make you feel like a Classroom Pro—ready to spread the word of its power throughout the school halls.

Think of Google Classroom as Your Classroom Hub of Learning

Usually, Google Classroom is the first tech tool that teachers gravitate toward because it is the hub for classroom work and organization. It is here that teachers post announcements and organize student assignments. Students know that if they have a question about assignments and due dates, they can turn to Google Classroom for quick answers. Savvy teachers can also create learning modules so that students—even those who are absent—can easily locate assignments and turn them in or do them at their own pace. All this interaction helps teachers create a largely paperless workspace and students stay up-to-date.

To Get Started With Google Classroom

⇨ Go to **classroom.google.com**

Only students and teachers who are in the same Google domain have access to the same Google Classroom hubs. This makes the work you do in Google Classroom private only to your school or district's students, parents, and staff. This is a safe space for students to email the teacher with questions and concerns.

⇨ **Note:** If you want to join someone's public Google Classroom for your own professional development, you must use your personal Gmail address.

Once you are at Google Classroom, you can create your class by heading to the gray PLUS button and selecting Create a Class. Google will assign a default theme to your class, but you can select the Theme option and personalize each classroom page with unique color and images—you can even use your own images. Each class page will have a unique code students will use to enter the class.

⇨ For a tutorial, go to **infused.link/playlist**

How Students Get Started

Students join the teacher's class by going to **classroom.google.com** and then clicking on the gray *plus* button in the upper right-hand corner. They select Join Class and type in the personal classroom code.

Getting to Know the Class Page

Google Classroom is a one-stop hub for class information that reduces the need for multiple cumbersome notebooks and planners. It goes a long way toward developing a paperless classroom.

For ease of use, each page is divided into four sections: Stream, Classwork, People and Grades.

STREAM

The Classroom default tab is the Stream tab, and it includes any class activities like announcements, assignments, or resources like articles, images, and videos a teacher can post to facilitate learning. The stream is chronological and allows teachers to schedule posts and get information out to students quickly. Students can scroll through the class stream by date to refer to assignments and resources they may have missed.

CLASSWORK

Select this tab to create assignments for students. Click on the Create button and choose the type of work you want to assign. This tab lets you do many things, like assign a due date or point values and even schedule posts in advance. You can organize work into topics to create things like learning modules that students might work on over a period of time or during project-based learning.

The Quiz option gives you a blank Google Form that you can populate with questions.

Click on Calendar to see scheduled assignments in Google Calendar.

PEOPLE

This tab tells you who is enrolled or connected to the class and allows you to communicate with them individually. This might include co-teachers.

You are the administrator for this page. You can add and remove students, and the email feature allows students to contact you with questions. The People page is also a great tool for encouraging digital citizenship. You can respond directly to constructive comments and mute students who need to improve in this area.

Parents can also be invited to connect to your Classroom to monitor their child's assignments and email you with questions.

GRADES

This is an online gradebook that allows the teacher to view grades across classes. Teachers can also input and modify grades on all assignments that have been assigned through Google Classroom.

What's more, if your school has an online district grade reporting platform like Aries or Schoology, it is highly likely that you can connect and send grades directly to that platform from your Google Classroom gradebook.

10 TEN TIPS FOR USING GOOGLE CLASSROOM

Differentiate Assignments: Google Classroom allows you to assign different or modified assignments to individual students. Teachers can even give groups their own unique assignments. To do this, in the assignment mode, click on All Students and select which students get a particular assignment.

Reuse Post: The reuse post allows you to take assignments from another one of your classes or archived classes and reuse them. You can modify the assignment to add new information or make any needed changes before reassigning.

Class Survey: Conduct a quick class survey by posting a question to the Stream page and give students a chance to thoughtfully reply—you can project this activity so students can see the responses of their classmates.

Background Colors: Are students writing a paper? When they turn in the work, have them select a background color for the page that corresponds to their stage in the draft process. This way, when you look at assignments in grid view, you can quickly and easily see where each student is in the process. For example, use orange for first drafts and green for the final draft. This idea comes from two great teachers in New York (@mahopacskiteam and @cauthersj). Examples of this strategy are in *The Chromebook Infused Classroom* Online Course, in case you want to learn more.

5 **Mobile App:** Use the mobile Classroom app to annotate documents or photos. The mobile app can also be used for those kids who have long bus rides and in transit or at after-school activities. The mobile app also gives students notifications.

6 **Stream Tab:** Using the Stream tab, you can tag students in a comment to help foster a richer conversation or get that student some important information.

7 **Topics:** Become a Topic Geek to Organize Your Classroom! Use Topics as a great organizational tool. To make learning modules or unit assignments, organize work into Topics by dragging and dropping to give your Classroom work a more organized and accessible structure. This tool even allows you to create learning modules that students can progress through at their own pace.

8 **Topics:** Make a tutorial Topic that houses math tutorials or history videos to help students who might need additional examples or were absent from class.

9 **Topics:** Create a 'notes' Topic where students can collaborate on notes together.

10 **Topics:** Use Topics to help keep Classroom from getting cluttered. Group assignments by date with corresponding resources.

Your Chromebook Superpowers

Meet the Apps and Extensions

@monicaisabelmtz

Adobe Spark
spark.adobe.com
graphics, video, and website design

Jamboard
Jamboard.google.com
collaborative digital whiteboard

Book Creator
app.bookcreator.com
digital book creator

Nearpod
nearpod.com
interactive lesson presentation tool

Buncee
app.edu.buncee.com
visual presentation creator

Pear Deck
peardeck.com
interactive formative tasks

Classcraft
classcraft.com
gaming platform

Quizizz
quizizz.com
gamified assessments

Edji
edji.it
collaborative reading app

Screencastify
screencastify.com
screen recording extension for Chrome

Flipgrid
flipgrid.com
video response platform

Seesaw
web.seesaw.me
digital learning journal

Genially
genial.ly
presentation / infographic creator

Socrative
socrative.com
assessment tool

Go Formative
goformative.com
assessment tool

TextHelp
texthelp.com
tools for reading, writing, and math

Google Keep
keep.google.com
note-taking and organization tool

Wakelet
wakelet.com
save, organize, and share web content

Hyperdocs
hyperdocs.co
blended learning lessons

WeVideo
wevideo.com
video creation tool

To download colored remixed versions of the graphics in this section for your school or teachers head to infused.link/20superpowers

YOUR
CHROMEBOOK
SUPERPOWERS
MEET THE APPS
AND EXTENSIONS

Holly Clark

Apps and extensions that will help you create a truly inspiring Infused Classroom!

This section is your tool kit—useful apps and extensions that are indispensable in a Chromebook Infused Classroom. Each section provides an overview, multiple uses for teachers and students, and a link to the actual app, costs, and online resources.

If a tool has made it into the section, you can be assured that it is educator-tested and highly recommended for relevance and adding value in *The Chromebook Infused Classroom.*

This section comes with a playlist that will help teachers get started with each of these learning tools!

ADOBE SPARK

spark.adobe.com

What is Adobe Spark?

It is a graphic design, video, and website creation app. Students can easily brand their creations so that their work has an individualized look with the school enterprise version of the app. Login with G Suite account.

What should you know about Adobe Spark?

✓ Add copyright free images or add your own in Spark Video, Pages, and Posts.

✓ Personalize the look of your videos, pages, and posts by adding your students' own unique branding.

✓ Projects automatically sync on all devices so you can work anywhere.

✓ As a bonus, it integrates seamlessly into Google Classroom and Google Drive!

Age levels?

Most-This app can work with all grade levels, but it is probably best starting about third grade, except for Spark Video, which can be used as early as kindergarten with some assistance.

Setup instructions: infused.link/playlist

What can teachers do with Adobe Spark?

☑ Create video responses templates and share with the class.

☑ Create back-to-school videos and pages for Meet-the-Teacher night.

☑ Create informational graphics for events.

☑ Create class websites.

☑ Create week-in-review videos.

☑ Create newsletters.

What does Adobe Spark cost?

Adobe Spark Free

Schools can sign up for the enterprise version, which is consistent with COPPA and FERPA. More information can be found at **spark.adobe.com/edu.**

What apps work great with Adobe Spark?

Book Creator—Video stories embedded in with illustrations created in Post

Flipgrid—Add the videos to a grid for feedback and curation.

Padlet—Easily publish posts, videos, and pages in a visual way.

Google Sites—Showcase creations in portfolios.

Seesaw—Reflect on creations and receive feedback.

Customize the game experience to meet their unique classroom and instructional needs.

Take it further with Adobe Spark

Create social media campaigns for school events.

Have students make spark videos to reflect on their learning and how they grew over time at the end-of-unit or end-of-year learning.

What can STUDENTS do with Adobe Spark?

1 Create a social media campaign.

2 Sight word videos.

3 Narrate five picture stories.

4 Six word summaries.

5 Multimedia biography reports.

6 Create digital citizenship pledge videos.

7 Video book reports.

8 Reflect on their learning.

9 Showcase learning in digital portfolios pages.

BOOK CREATOR

app.bookcreator.com

What is Book Creator?

It is an easy-to-use tool for making multimedia digital books and learning journals in any subject area.

What can teachers do with Book Creator?

- ☑ **Create their own library and invite students to join with a code.**
- ☑ **Create resources for students to engage with.**
- ☑ **Create template books for younger students to work from.**
- ☑ **Differentiate tasks for all ages and abilities.**
- ☑ **Engage reluctant writers by giving them wider options for writing— use images, speech-to-text, drawings, or record their voices.**
- ☑ **Publish student work beyond the classroom, giving students a wider audience for their work.**

What should you know about Book Creator?

- ✓ Create-Combine text, audio, video, drawings, photos and appsmash.
- ✓ Read-Have your book read to you in multiple languages, with word highlighting.
- ✓ Publish-Share your book online, download as an ePub file or print.

Age levels?

K-12

Setup instructions:
infused.link/playlist

What does Book Creator cost?

Book Creator Free	Book Creator Upgrade
Get one library and 40 books	Three libraries with 180 books ($60 per year) or unlimited libraries with 1,000 books ($120 per year). Upgraded accounts get real-time collaboration and other admin features.

What apps work great with Book Creator?

Google Apps—Embed maps and YouTube videos, add files from Drive, or share to Google Classroom.

Embed content created in other apps: Adobe Spark, Explain Everything, Soundtrap, Flipgrid, and lots more (anything with an embed code).

➤ Take it further with FlipBook Creator

Work on a book together—Collaborate with another classroom in your school or from around the world.

Create a range of books and publish the whole library online to showcase your students' work. Embed that library on your class blog.

Create a "Choose Your Own Adventure" story by hyperlinking pages with multiple options to plot your way through the book.

What can STUDENTS do with Book Creator?

1 Create all kinds of books, e.g., comics, poetry, stories.

2 Demonstrate their understanding, e.g., create their own math textbooks, social studies research journals, or science reports.

3 Document their learning, e.g., create portfolios of work, reading response journals, or historical timelines.

4 Create Learning Journals that show learning over time. These journals can be a way to keep track of learning and used at the end to demonstrate knowledge. This can be a way to replace multiple choice tests.

BUNCEE

app.edu.buncee.com

What is Buncee?

Buncee is a platform that fosters creation through its easy-to-use, all-in-one platform. It allows students, teachers, and administrators to easily create and share visual presentations.

What should you know about Buncee?

✓ It comes with tools like 3-D graphics, recorded video, and drawing. Formative tools such as MC questions and FRQ are available.

✓ Students can start with a blank slide presentation or choose from over thousands of templates.

✓ Buncee is a one-stop shop to build media-rich lessons, reports, newsletters, presentations and so much more.

Age levels?

Most*–This app can work with all grade levels, but it is probably best starting in the primary grades (first through fifth).

What can teachers do with Buncee?

☑ Create Buncee study guides.

☑ Create virtual field trips.

☑ Create interactive practice tests and quizzes.

☑ Create diagrams and anchor charts.

☑ Create interactive maps and timelines.

☑ Create self-checking quizzes, HW, and assignments.

What does Buncee cost?

Buncee Free	Buncee Upgrade
It offers a limited thirty-day trial with the ability to create three Buncees and access to graphics and templates.	Premium gives unlimited Buncees, video and audio recording, ability to upload files, and clip or stitch. Classroom adds ability to include free response and multiple choice questioning.

Setup instructions: infused.link/playlist

What apps work great with Buncee?

Flipgrid—Add a Buncee to a topic.

PebbleGo—Mash up with Buncee research templates.

Khan Academy is embedded.

Take it further with Buncee

Try flipping your classroom lesson by embedding tutorial videos and example problems into a Buncee lesson. Modify for student ability or level.

Create an interactive word wall that the entire class can contribute to.

Fluency journals: Have students create a fluency journal using the recording tool in Buncee. Instead of just marking down their speed and accuracy, they can demonstrate it.

What can STUDENTS do with Buncee?

1 Publish writing with audio read-aloud.

2 Create vocabulary journals.

3 Create book bento boxes.

4 Create translation journals, translating native language into the language they're learning.

5 Conduct interactive science experiments and reports.

6 Create engaging biographies.

7 Visualize words problems in math.

CLASSCRAFT

classcraft.com

What is Classcraft?

Classcraft uses the cultural phenomenon of video games to help educators drive measurable academic performance, non-cognitive skills development, and school climate. By blending students' physical and virtual learning, the program reframes their progress in school as a game they play together throughout the year.

What should you know about Classcraft?

✓ It is highly customizable and can be used with any subject and grade level.

✓ It offers multiple purposes, such as classroom management, personalized learning, SEL, and PBIS.

✓ It integrates seamlessly with Google Classroom and Google Drive.

Age levels?

Most-This program can work with all grade levels-but probably best starting about <u>third grade.</u>

What can teachers do with Classcraft?

 Use a powerful set of classroom management and curriculum design tools to engage students through the power of games.

☑ Teach the whole child in a more effective way by using motivating gaming principles to supplement existing teaching practices.

☑ Create a classroom environment that's more fun and stimulating while personalizing instruction, fostering collaboration and SEL, and empowering students.

☑ Customize the game experience to meet their unique classroom and instructional needs.

Setup instructions: infused.link/playlist

What does Classcraft cost?

Classcraft Free	Classcraft Premium	School & District
Unlimited classes and students, includes gamified classroom management, customizable characters, and parent features	Unlimited classes and students, $8/month for a full year (or $12 month-to-month), all game components (Quests, Class Tools, Student Analytics, etc.)	By quote, includes enhanced security, admin control and support, School Dashboard, School Climate and Engagement Indexes, etc.

What apps work great with Classcraft?

Google Drive and Google Classroom—to upload or submit assignments and convert grades to game points

Microsoft OneDrive— to upload and submit assignments

Take it further with Classcraft

Use Quests for self-paced personalized learning, differentiated learning, and blended learning.

Use Boss Battles for formative assessment.

Use Class Tools like the Timer, Stopwatch, and Random Events to pace class activities or make them more interactive.

Use the Student Analytics to assess a record of student behavior and academic performance compared to the class average.

Use Gold Pieces to reward students for going above and beyond and help them unlock new gear for their characters.

Use Parent Accounts to engage parents and extend the game experience to the home by letting parents award points for doing chores or homework.

Use the School Dashboard to get deeper analytics and insights and measure school climate and engagement via powerful indexes.

What can STUDENTS do with Classcraft?

1 Play in teams and achieve success through collaboration.

2 Earn points for positive behaviors and teamwork.

3 Unlock real privileges (customizable), such as getting to eat in class or getting extra time on an exam.

4 Create an avatar (game character) and customize them with unique gear and pets.

5 Enjoy a more inclusive, supportive, and fun classroom culture.

6 Become better learners through positive reinforced habits and increased engagement and motivation.

EDJI ···························
edji.it

What is Edji?

It is a reading tool that inspires engagement! Edji turns reading into an engaging, collaborative experience.

What should you know about Edji?

✓ It comes with three different comment types: audio, emoji, and text.

✓ Students don't need an account.

✓ It works with text, images, GIFs, PDFs, or a combination of these.

Age levels?

MOST*–This app has been used in kindergarten classrooms to create associations between phonemes and images and in college classes to discuss supply chain management.

What can teachers do with Edji?

☑ Share graphs, maps, and charts for social studies, math or science.

☑ Integrate song lyrics into history or poetry lessons.

☑ Turn a news article into a platform for practicing close reading.

☑ Upload a PDF of a book or short story so students can read together and discuss remotely.

☑ See which words and paragraphs generate the most interest (or challenges) for students.

☑ See real-time data on what students are reading, thinking, and discussing.

☑ Differentiate based on the needs of the class and individual students.

Setup instructions: infused.link/playlist

What does Edji cost?

Edji Free	Edji Upgrade
Two readings	Unlimited groups and readings. Access to the Reading Recap, Individual Student View, unlimited PDF uploads, and new features.

What apps work great with Edji?

Flipgrid—Students can post URL links to a Grid video into a text comment (so it's kind of like a video comment).

GIPHY—Because Edji supports GIFs, it's a great way to show processes and change over time by including a GIF.

Google Draw—Create custom images or graphic organizers to insert into Edji

Take it further with Edji

Edji archaeology—Add high-resolution images of historical artifacts and ask students to think like an archaeologist and make inferences based on the item.

Gallery walk—Students can "post" their ideas on gallery boards without needing any sticky notes.

What can STUDENTS do with Edji?

1 Use it to analyze a text for cause and effect clue words, point of view, details about the setting, important details for the main idea, and more!

2 Use it to make inferences using text or compelling images.

3 Practice looking at and thinking about text features.

4 Create read aloud audio books using audio comments.

5 Reply to one another.

FLIPGRID

flipgrid.com

What should you know about Flipgrid?

✓ Teachers create discussion prompts.

✓ Students record video responses.

✓ Use responses to foster student thinking, understanding, reflection, and social learning.

Age levels?

☆ This app is great for all levels.

What does Flipgrid cost?

Free for everyone!

▶ What is Flipgrid?

Flipgrid is a video response and discussion platform.

It allows students to develop and share their voice and thinking using videos and various app smashes.

What can teachers do with Flipgrid?

☑ Post questions that allow them to hear from every student in their class.

☑ Develop protocols that allow students to make their journey of understanding visible.

☑ Develop a sense of community.

☑ Connect with other educators from around the world.

☑ Allow for authentic reflection.

☑ Give their students a voice.

☑ Help students develop their metacognitive skills.

Setup instructions: infused.link/playlist

What apps work great with Flipgrid?

ChatterPix

Snapchat or Instagram

Adobe Spark

Wakelet

▶ Take it further with Flipgrid

Try Grid Pals and connect with other classes.

Create magic by turning any video into an Augmented Reality experience using Flipgrid AR.

Use the Disco Library to discover ideas from fellow educators and education partners.

Add a co-pilot to collaborate with another teacher.

Create a Mixtape to chart student growth throughout a unit.

Host a YouTube-like video in a safe environment.

What can STUDENTS do with Flipgrid?

1 Practice expressing themselves articulately.

2 Explain their thinking.

3 Connect globally.

4 Provide feedback to their peers.

5 Learn to be better speakers.

6 Share their work.

7 Ask their own questions.

infused.link/camerashy

FORMATIVE

goformative.com

What is Formative?

It is a site that allows teachers to build their own assessments ("formatives") and view student responses in real time. Teachers can also upload pre-existing resources and add questions to them, grab pre-existing formatives from the library, and embed almost any other site into their formatives.

What should you know about Formative?

- ✅ Everything continually auto saves, including student responses and updates, immediately on the teacher's screen.

- ✅ Teachers can tag standards to questions and track student progress against those standards over time in the site's Tracker.

- ✅ With Premium, teachers can post assignments to Google Classroom with one click and pass grades back too.

Age levels?

- ✩ Most*—This app can work with all grade levels, but it is probably best starting about third grade.

Setup instructions: infused.link/playlist

What can teachers do with Formative?

- ✅ Check for understanding at any point in a lesson.

- ✅ Facilitate class discussion by projecting responses (with names hidden) onto a smart board or screen.

- ✅ Use for class work—the teacher dashboard shows how far each student is progressing through the assignment, allowing teachers to intervene when they see students stalling or struggling.

- ✅ Use for homework. (Formative does the grading work, enabling teachers to see, before the day starts, how they may need to adjust their instruction.)

- ✅ Use to flip their classrooms (or for e-learning days) by embedding videos, text, other media, and sites and tools like Flipgrid into a formative and add questions.

What does Formative cost?

Formative Free

It includes unlimited formatives, real-time responses, basic grading tools, and teacher-to-student feedback.

Formative Upgrade

Premium includes advanced question types and grading tools, more assign options, student-to-teacher feedback, full Google Classroom integration, and more.

Take it further with Formative

Assign a blank formative to students at the beginning of class and add questions or content to it as class progresses. (Any changes the teacher makes immediately update on the student side.)

Track student growth over a semester or year by tagging standards to questions.

Collaborate with colleagues to build common formative assessments together (team, school, and district sub-scriptions).

Use Formative for PD by assigning a formative to guests (no login required).

What can STUDENTS do with Formative?

1 Show their thinking with Show Your Work and explain orally with Audio Response questions.

2 See their scores and the correct answers instantly or when they finish a formative (depending on the teacher's settings).

3 Upload photos and screenshots of other work into a Show-Your-Work question.

4 Ask their teacher questions and respond to feedback (premium subscriptions).

5 Track their own progress against standards.

GENIALLY

genial.ly

What is Genially?

Genially is a content creation tool that helps students and teachers bring their learning resources to life. Use Genially as your all-in-one online tool to create stunning presentations, interactive images, infographics, posters, quizzes, etc. and enrich them with interactivity and animation effects in seconds.

What should you know about Genially?

✓ Fresh new templates are added weekly, so you never run out.

✓ Add audio to your creations.

✓ Share to Google Classroom with one click.

Age levels?

Most*—This app can be used by teachers and students to create learning resources and complete projects for any age level.

What can teachers do with Genially?

Teachers can create a great variety of interactive learning resources, including:

- ☑ Gamified experiences and escape rooms
- ☑ Interactive images and lessons
- ☑ Posters
- ☑ Infographics
- ☑ Share to Google Classroom
- ☑ Add and record audio

What does Genially cost?

Genially Free

Sign-up for free and access dozens of free templates and resources. Unlimited creations and views!

Genially Upgrade

Upgrade to access premium templates. Download your creations as PDF and JPG files, and organize your content in folders. Import your slides to bring them to life, remove the watermark and enjoy collaborative features and more sharing options.

Setup instructions: infused.link/playlist

What apps work great with Genially?

Google Classroom   Padlet

Flipgrid   Seesaw

Wakelet

1 Create amazing demonstrations of learning, from presentations to infographics.

2 Collaborate easily with peers when needed.

3 Record their thinking and learning on top of the slides.

Take it further with Genially

Create Infographics. Genially is a great tool for data visualization. Check out this tutorial infused.link/genially

Find Inspiration examples by real educators in the inspiration section of the tool.

Work collaboratively with your students and other teachers.

Remove the Genially watermark and personalize your creations with your school brand, or your own.

GOOGLE KEEP

keep.google.com

What is Google Keep?

Google Keep allows students to capture notes, label, and color-code them, share them with other students, and access them from any computer, phone, or tablet.

Setup instructions: infused.link/playlist

Age levels?

All age levels are good, but it is probably best to start in about <u>third grade</u>.

What does Google Keep Cost?

Free with your Google Account

What can teachers do with Google Keep?

- ☑ Help students learn to organize their tasks by adding them to a shared note in Google Keep.

- ☑ Show students how to organize their research.

- ☑ Help students keep track of homework by adding it to Google Keep and sharing with parents.

- ☑ Create drawings in Google Keep and share the visual example with students.

- ☑ Create voice notes for audio feedback to share with students.

- ☑ Use Google Keep to give students feedback on their Google Docs and Google Slides!

Take it further with Google Keep

Check out this video by Matt Miller on Ninja Tricks for Google Keep: infused.link/keeptips

What can
STUDENTS
do with Google Keep?

1 Keep track of their ideas and tasks in one place.

2 Share notes with other students during group assignments.

3 Create voice notes to capture thoughts easily on the go.

4 View their Google Keep on the side bar of their Google Docs. Then, drag and drop notes into Google Docs.

5 Use the search bar to easily find notes.

6 Learn how color coding can be used to organize individual class notes and ideas.

7 Students can set location-based reminders to do homework when they get home.

8 Use the mobile app to annotate.

9 Take pictures of handwritten text and Google Keep AI will turn it to text.

HYPERDOCS

hyperdocs.co

What is HyperDocs?

HyperDocs are a way to package digital lessons in order to create quality inquiry-based learning experiences. Teachers design these lessons including specific elements tailored to meet the needs of their students. Once students access the lessons, teachers can deliver the instruction, blended learning style, in order to meet each student's need in the classroom.

What should you know about HyperDocs?

✓ A HyperDoc is not a webquest or a doc with links. Its effectiveness and purpose is based on the intentions of the person who created the lesson.

✓ HyperDocs are not a program; there is not one right way to make them. Instead, they enable teachers to design learning experiences rather than just assign work.

✓ HyperDocs have the potential to shift the way teachers deliver instruction and the way students experience learning.

Age levels?

All levels including Administration

What can teachers do with HyperDocs?

☑ Design lessons to meet the specific needs of students in the classroom by including web tools, links, videos, and clear instructions.

☑ Use HyperDocs as a sub plan, giving the plans to the students rather than the substitute.

☑ Create lessons from scratch using a template or by remixing a lesson already created.

☑ Find lessons at teachersgiveteachers.net, @tsgivets, or on the HyperDoc Facebook page, where an active community of educators is there to support various needs.

☑ Create HyperDocs as needed to solve a learning goal, not for every lesson.

What does HyperDocs cost?

HyperDocs Free	HyperDocs Upgrade
Created with Google apps, these lessons are shared for free at TeachersgiveTeachers.net.	HyperDocs Academy—Learn more about how to create and deliver instruction at hyperdocs.co.

Setup instructions: infused.link/playlist

What apps work great with HyperDocs?

G Suite apps—A HyperDoc can be created on any of the apps.

Microsoft OneNote—Digital lessons can be created using this infinite canvas and collaborative tool.

Apps for digital collaboration—Padlet, Wakelet, Mural.co, Flipgrid

Apps for creating—Adobe Spark Video, WeVideo, Adobe Spark Post

Take it further with HyperDocs

Create PBL lessons packaged in one convenient method and accessible to all students.

Build community with collaborative activities built into a HyperDoc lesson.

Design with UDL strategies in order to meet the needs of all students.

Create learning experiences that purposefully integrate quality activities for lasting learning beyond the assessment.

What can STUDENTS do with HyperDocs?

1 Build inquiry skills by exploring content before teacher explanation.

2 Build agency for their learning by figuring out tasks based on how the HyperDoc is designed.

3 Experience active learning by navigating the expectations built into a HyperDoc lesson.

4 Connect and collaborate with other students through web tools included in the HyperDoc.

5 Be set up for successful learning experiences based on the organizational features of all they need, packaged in one place.

6 Share their work efficiently through links packaged on a HyperDoc.

7 Work at their own pace and continue learning with classmates if they are absent for an extended period of time.

8 Create HyperDoc lessons as a way to show what they know, providing learning content for their classmates.

JAMBOARD

jamboard.google.com

What is Jamboard?

Jamboard is a free collaborative, digital whiteboard that makes it easy to create without boundaries and share ideas in real time. Jamboard has taken the idea of whiteboards and moved them to the cloud.

What can teachers do with Jamboard?

- ☑ **Create a template and push out through Google Classroom**
- ☑ **Insert documents and slides easily into the whiteboard**
- ☑ **Draw, write and erase**
- ☑ **Add sticky notes and images**
- ☑ **Change the background for graphing paper**
- ☑ **Create multiple frames and boards all on the same screen**
- ☑ **Invite others to collaborate by sharing a link or inviting via email**
- ☑ **Export as an image or PDF**
- ☑ **Use Screencastify to explain content and share the recording**

What does Jamboard cost?

Free: Google Core product

Note: Your admin will need to turn it on

Age levels?

All levels, including administration

What can students do with Jamboard?

1 Collaborate on projects or collaboratively Sketchnote

2 Draw, doodle, do math problems and music sheets

3 Collaborate, create, brainstorm, plan (e.g., design thinking)

4 Have students record their thinking using Screencastify

5 Use shape/letter recognition

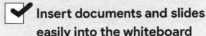

Setup instructions: infused.link/playlist

Special thanks to Chrystal Hoe @cehoerun for her input on this

NEARPOD

nearpod.com

What is Nearpod?

It is an interactive lesson presentation tool. Teachers and students can use Nearpod to create and share presentations that include multiple formative assessment options, virtual tours, 3-D images, simulations, websites, and games. Students join the teacher's presentation with a code and interact with the presentation on their screen.

What does Nearpod cost?

Silver (Free)–Add polls, simulations, 3-D objects, quizzes, and more to lessons.

Gold ($120/year)–Includes Silver features plus the option to add virtual field trips, web content, embed YouTube videos, and multiple On the Fly features to lessons.

Age levels?

Preschool through college

What can teachers do with Nearpod?

- ☑ Upload and "nearpodize" existing Google Slides presentations using the website or Chrome extension.
- ☑ Poll students to gather information.
- ☑ Use the "draw it" feature to annotate slides.
- ☑ Embed formative assessment to gauge student learning.
- ☑ Take students on virtual field trips.
- ☑ Progress through lessons without being tied to a desktop.
- ☑ Share lessons anywhere by launching a live lesson.

What can students do with Nearpod?

1 Interact with lessons and presentations.

2 Create their own Nearpod lessons to present information and collaborate with their peers.

3 View information on their individual devices.

4 Share their opinions on and understanding of content through polling, questions, and other embedded activities.

Setup instructions: infused.link/playlist

PEAR DECK

peardeck.com

What is Pear Deck?

Pear Deck was founded by educators on a mission to help teachers engage every student every day. With solutions rooted in active learning and formative assessment, they make it easy for you to connect with learners of every age and ability.

What should you know about Pear Deck?

✓ It is the fastest way to transform presentations into classroom conversations using formative assessments and interactive questions.

✓ It seamlessly integrates with Google Slides (and Microsoft PPT).

✓ Don't start from scratch–use an existing lesson or our Template Library!

Age levels?

Pear Deck is a platform for all learners regardless of the grade-level or subject area!

What can teachers do with Pear Deck?

☑ Make lessons interactive by using the Teacher Dashboard.

☑ Add interactive elements to each slide by choosing to add text, choice, number options, push out web content, allow students to draw, or have them drag content to the right place.

☑ View all of the responses on the teacher dashboard.

☑ Keep this information private or share it out with the entire class by projecting the answers on the screen.

☑ Teachers can also go back later to look more in depth at how each student responded.

What does Pear Deck cost?

peardeck.com/pricing

For 3 FREE Months head to **peardeck.com/holly-clark**

Setup instructions: infused.link/playlist

What apps work great with Pear Deck?

Google Apps

➤ Take it further with Pear Deck

Have students use the drawing feature to solve a math problem or draw the inside of a cell.

Use the "End of lesson" template to have students do a brain dump or exit card at the end of a lesson.

Use the thumb up and down feature to ask students how well they have comprehended a difficult piece of information or concept.

What can STUDENTS do with Pear Deck?

1 Have a voice, engage, and actively participate in class without having to raise their hand.

2 Students head to joinpd.com on their device and use the teacher-generated code to get started.

3 When appropriate, students can compare their responses and comment or compare answers with those of the entire class.

4 Do asynchronous learning in student-paced mode.

SOCRATIVE

socrative.com

What is Socrative?

Socrative is a response system that allows teachers to ask different types of questions and see responses in real time. Open-ended questions allow teachers to make student thinking visible quickly without the need for lots of preparation.

What should you know about Socrative?

✓ What should you know about Socrative?

✓ Students can access from any device, mobile or web

✓ Get quick access to reports with students answers in Google Drive

✓ Access to instant feedback

Age levels?

Most—this book recommends use with third grade students and beyond.

What can teachers do with Socrative?

✔ **Create quick check-ins with students using open ended questions.**

✔ **Share student answers on-screen so students can learn from each other.**

✔ **Create interactive and engaging challenges through Space Race: In Space Race ships move along screen as students answer correctly.**

✔ **See data in spreadsheets and keep track of learning over time.**

✔ **Share and collaborate on assessments with other teachers**

What does Socrative cost?

Socrative Free	Socrative Pro Version
The free version is really good, and what I use.	$59.99 a year includes 20 private or public rooms, 20 activities at once, Space Race countdown timer and roster import via CSV or Excel.

Setup instructions: infused.link/playlist

What apps work great with Socrative?

Google Drive

►Take it further with Socrative

Create personalized assessments.

Use quick check-ins to check for understanding in real time.

Create exploratory Space Races before the unit to have students investigate information before you start learning content.

QUIZIZZ
quizizz.com

What should you know about Quizizz?

✓ Teachers can create their own quizzes or use the millions of teacher-created quizzes available on the platform.

✓ Teachers can share quizzes that students can play live or asynchronously on the platform.

✓ All quizzes are automatically graded, and teachers can access data for games they host.

Age levels?

K–12

What is Quizizz?

This is a student-paced learning platform that uses gamification to make academic and non-academic topics a lot more interesting for learners.

Setup instructions:
infused.link/playlist

What does Quizizz cost?

Quizizz Free
Quizizz is completely free to use

What apps work great with Quizizz?

Google Classroom   Schoology

Remind   Canvas

What can teachers do with Quizizz?

- ✔ Create quizzes on any topic.

- ✔ Choose from a variety of question types (Fill-in-the-Blank, Polls, Checkbox and Open-Ended questions).

- ✔ Teleport questions from existing teacher-created quizzes into their own quiz.

- ✔ Play live games with their students, either in the classroom or remotely (with or without a conferencing tool).

- ✔ Conduct solo-player and team games with students.

- ✔ Fast and Curious EduProtocol with Quizizz infused.link/quizizz.

▶ Take it further with Quizizz

Use cool gamification settings like Power-ups or Name Factory to make practice more interesting

What can STUDENTS do with Quizizz?

1 Play quizzes shared by their teachers on their own device (mobile, desktop or tablet).

2 Pick from millions of quizzes on a variety of topics and play practice games on their own.

3 Host games and play with their friends.

4 Create their own quizzes to practice and study.

5 Use quiz flashcards to study before they attempt a quiz (Flashcards are available for every quiz on the platform).

SCREENCASTIFY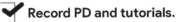

screencastify.com

What is Screencastify?

It is a screen recording extension for Chrome. Have students record their screen, embed their webcams, and use annotation tools to make their thinking visible. All videos save to Google Drive.

What can teachers do with Screencastify?

- ☑ **Leave tutorials on how to use an app, solve a problem, or complete a HyperDoc.**
- ☑ **Leave lesson plans for substitute teachers.**
- ☑ **Leave verbal comments on papers or projects.**
- ☑ **Record PD and tutorials.**
- ☑ **Record videos for parents.**
- ☑ **Create Vlogs.**
- ☑ **Record Whiteboard videos for detailed explanations.**
- ☑ **Teachers can create a magic link for students to submit videos to Google Classroom. For more info: infused.link/submit**

What should you know about Screencastify?

- ✓ Comes with a set of markup tools
- ✓ Record offline and sync when back online
- ✓ Integrates seamlessly with Google Classroom and Google Drive

Age levels?

Most*-This app can work with all grade levels but is probably best starting about third grade.

Setup instructions:
infused.link/playlist

What does Screencastify cost?

Screencastify Free	Screencastify Upgrade
Record free up to five minutes.	Unlimited includes unlimited recording length and access to the browser-based editor.

What apps work great with Screencastify?

Google Apps

Scratch—create scratch journals

Book Creator—embed into books

Flipgrid—Add the screencastifies to a grid.

Jamboard—bring tutorials into a board

➤ Take it further with Screencastify

HyperDoc instructions and explanations

HyperDoc reflections

Book Creator—Add tutorials made in Screencastify (by students or the teacher) into a help book for students.

Have students make slides of end-of-unit or end-of-year learning and use Screencastify to explain their learning and reflect on how it grew over the time period (video example: bit.ly/screencastifyexample).

What can STUDENTS do with Screencastify?

1 Students can take the Screencastify Jr. Course.

2 Student generated tutorial videos.

3 Show how they solved a problem with step-by-step instructions.

4 Record a Tour Builder project or My Maps tour.

5 Practice presentations.

6 Record reading fluency.

7 Narrate Slide Decks.

8 Summarize Vlogs.

9 Dub a video—mute existing video and record with your own narration (credit @EricCurts).

10 Reflect on their learning with screencasts students turn in to Google Classroom.

SEESAW

web.seesaw.me

What is Seesaw?

Seesaw is a platform for fostering meaningful student engagement. It combines student portfolios, family communication, and an activity library for teachers.

What should you know about Seesaw?

✓ Seesaw works on all types of devices (including Chromebooks, iPads, Tablets, etc.), and it works well whether you have shared or one-to-one devices in your classroom.

✓ Seesaw is used in over 200,000 classrooms, 150+ countries, and one out of two schools in the US.

✓ Seesaw was a 2018 Top Pick for Learning by Common Sense Education

Age levels?

Seesaw is great for all classrooms grades K-12.

What can teachers do with Seesaw?

☑ Give students a space for ownership and choice.

☑ Celebrate and recognize student progress.

☑ Spark conversation centered on student learning with families.

☑ Gain insights to meet your students where they are.

☑ Get inspiration and ideas for your classroom in the Seesaw Activity Library.

☑ Organize student work and assessment checks in folders.

What does Seesaw cost?

Seesaw Free	Seesaw Plus	Seesaw for Schools
Seesaw's three core features—student portfolios, family communication, and the activity library—are free for teachers.	For $120 per year, teachers can subscribe for advanced tools for assessment and better collaboration with peers.	Seesaw for Schools is a paid subscription service for schools and districts.

Setup instructions: infused.link/playlist

What apps work great with Seesaw?

Happy app smashing! Seesaw pairs well with hundreds of apps you're using in your classroom. Students share links, videos, photos, and other work from other apps right into Seesaw so families can see it. Be sure to try Seesaw with these apps:

DoInk

Book Creator

Pic Collage

Buncee

Adobe Spark

ChatterPix

Shadow Puppet EDU

Flipgrid

Google Apps

▶ Take it further with Seesaw

Visit the Seesaw Activity Library for ideas and inspiration.

100 Ways Students Use Seesaw Printable at infused.link/100seesaw.

Check out FREE webinars at web.seesaw.me/pds.

What can STUDENTS do with Seesaw?

1 Use powerful creative tools in the Seesaw app to create and capture learning in any subject area.

2 Take pictures, record voice while drawing, annotate work with labels, and much more to show your thinking.

3 Choose the creative tools that allow them to show what they know in the way that works best for the learner.

4 Show learning in math by narrating thinking while solving a problem.

5 Record reading for fluency.

6 Use the record feature to make student thinking and learning visible.

7 See student progress over time.

8 Practice digital citizenship skills by interacting with other students in polite ways.

9 Share learning with families.

TEXTHELP

texthelp.com

What is TextHelp?

Text help is a collection of immensely helpful assistive technology apps that work with Google Chrome and G Suite to support students. They are: **Read Write, Equatio, Fluency Tutor**, and **WriQ**.

What should you know about TextHelp?

Read&Write for Google Chrome™ provides personalized support to make documents, web pages and common file types in Google Drive (including: Google Docs, Slides, PDF, and EPUB) more accessible. It's designed to help everyone engage with digital content in a way that suits his/her abilities and learning styles.

EquatIO allows teachers to easily add equations, formulas, graphs and more to G Suite for Education apps. Use the toolbar to create, explore and collaborate. Use EquatIO's prediction, speech input, handwriting recognition, and more to support students in digital math and STEM classes.

Fluency Tutor makes reading aloud more fun and satisfying for students who need extra practice. It's especially useful for emerging and reluctant readers, as well as students learning English as a second language.

WriQ is a writing achievement tool designed to accelerate student writing proficiency. It allows educators to quickly assess student writing and provides practical data to easily monitor progress. Students get immediate and clear feedback on writing with nudges and badges.

Age levels?

All classrooms grades K–12.

What can teachers do with TextHelp?

- ☑ **Read&Write —Give your learners the support they need to understand lesson content. Provide emerging and struggling readers with the motivation and support to progress in tangible leaps and bounds.**

- ☑ **EquatIO—Provide equal access to math and STEM content for students with learning disabilities or visual impairments**

- ☑ **Fluency Tutor—Assign built-in reading passages and comprehension questions. Create custom content to share with students**

- ☑ **WriQ—Assess documents with detailed and relevant feedback. Track important metrics, including vocabulary maturity, time-on-task, accuracy and spelling, grammar and punctuation errors.**

What does TextHelp cost?

TextHelp Free

Each app has a different price structure for the upgraded version for students. Your IT Admin can look into these upgrades, but all apps are FREE for teachers to use!

Setup instructions: infused.link/playlist

What should you know about TextHelp?

Read&Write One toolbar leads to powerful support tools to help students gain confidence in reading, writing, studying and research.

EquatIO has an integrated web app that can be accessed through the G Suite or by visiting equatio.texthelp.com to design digital assignments.

Fluency Tutor comes with nearly 500 free reading passages that contain comprehension questions leveled at specific Lexiles.

WriQ allows teachers to assess writing faster and more equitably with built in rubrics, customized for grades 1–12, in three categories: Narrative, Informative, Opinion.

What apps work great with TextHelp?

Most G Suite apps, including Google Classroom, and websites including some LMS like Canvas and Schoology.

Take it further with TextHelp

Create PBL lessons packaged in one convenient method and accessible to all students.

Build community with collaborative activities built into a HyperDoc lesson.

Design with UDL strategies in order to meet the needs of all students.

Create learning experiences that purposefully integrate quality activities for lasting learning beyond the assessment.

What can STUDENTS do with TextHelp?

1 Read&Write—Text-to-speech allows students to follow along with words, passages, or whole documents read aloud with easy-to-follow dual color highlighting. Text and Picture Dictionaries help users to understand words through written or visual explanations.

2 EquatIO—Engage digitally in math with no tricky or complicated languages or coding to learn. Understand and engage with math concepts through active learning.

3 Fluency Tutor—Listen to assigned passages with text-to-speech technology. Look up words with a picture dictionary, talking dictionary, and translator. Practice reading passages by speaking into a computer mic. Create reading passages from websites and submit recordings for feedback.

4 WriQ—Track writing fluency in bursts, see a word cloud of academic keywords, earn badges, see detailed feedback in the extension.

WEVIDEO

wevideo.com

What is WeVideo?

It is an easy-to-use tool to allow students to create and show learning in any subject with video.

What should you know about WeVideo?

✓ It is an all-in-one media creation tool set (videos of all types, greenscreen, screen recording, podcasting, stock library, etc.).

✓ It is built for schools.

✓ It allows deep, comprehensive integration with the Google education ecosystem (Docs, Drive, Classroom, Chromebooks, or domain sync).

Age levels?

All grade levels

What can teachers do with WeVideo?

 Utilize the platform for collaboration and research.

 Create learning experiences that promote creativity and innovation.

 Provide structure for storytelling, reflection, and feedback.

What does WeVideo cost?

Varies
Classroom, building, and district options

Setup instructions: infused.link/playlist

What apps work great with WeVideo?

Google Docs—Students collaborate on their script for the video.

Google Slides—Build a storyboard/ picture script.

Book Creator—Add tutorials made in WeVideo into a help book for students.

Flipgrid—Input created videos to Flipgrid grids.

► Take it further with WeVideo

Ask students to create a video to show evidence that they not only understand the learning goal but have mastered the learning goal.

Include routines and procedures to be uploaded for spiral viewing.

Record lessons and upload to Google Classroom or other LMS for student interaction.

Digital storytelling

Student reflection of learning

Flipped lessons

Create a school-wide film festival.

Digital portfolios

What can STUDENTS do with WeVideo?

1 Collaborate with each other in one movie project.

2 Utilize the greenscreen.

3 Create vlogs.

4 Record their screens.

5 Reflection on their thinking.

6 Share their voice through storytelling.

7 Create four shot story summaries.

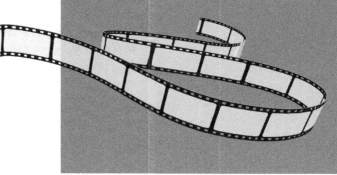

SLIDES MANIA

slidesmania.com

▶ What is Slides Mania?

This website is full of amazing slides templates you can download and share with students. This is a treasure trove for educators!

Find slides that mimic *Time Magazine* to other incredible educational examples—you will love this resource and find it so helpful for inspiring student creation.

BRUSH NINJA

Brush.ninja

▶ What is Brush Ninja?

This new app has not been around long enough for a full section.

Brush Ninja is a fun tool that students can use to learn about animation, to illustrate the concepts and ideas, or to make their presentations more interesting. Alternatively it can be a fun, free way for teachers to creatively present ideas to their students (from brush.ninja site).

elevatebooksedu.com

The Google Infused Classroom

A Guidebook to Making Thinking Visible and Amplifying Student Voice

By Holly Clark and Tanya Avrith

This beautifully designed book offers guidance on using technology to design instruction that allows students to show their thinking, demonstrate their learning, and share their work (and voices!) with authentic audiences. *The Google Infused Classroom* will equip you to empower your students to use technology in meaningful ways that prepare them for the future.

The Microsoft Infused Classroom

A Guidebook to Making Thinking Visible and Amplifying Student Voice

By Holly Clark and Tanya Avrith

Packed with ideas you can use in your classroom tomorrow, *The Microsoft Infused Classroom*, equips you to use powerful tools that put learning first. Edtech experts led by Holly Clark and Tanya Avrith show you how to use technology to increase engagement in your classroom and provide authentic opportunities for students to share their work and their voice.

Dive into Inquiry

Amplify Learning and Empower Student Voice

By Trevor MacKenzie

Dive into Inquiry beautifully marries the voice and choice of inquiry with the structure and support required to optimize learning. With *Dive into Inquiry* you'll gain an understanding of how to best support your learners as they shift from a traditional learning model into the inquiry classroom where student agency is fostered and celebrated each and every day.

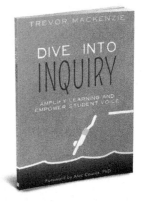

Inquiry Mindset

Nurturing the Dreams, Wonders, and Curiosities of Our Youngest Learners

By Trevor MacKenzie and Rebecca Bathurst-Hunt

Inquiry Mindset offers a highly accessible journey through inquiry in the younger years. Learn how to empower your students, increase engagement, and accelerate learning by harnessing the power of curiosity. With practical examples and a step-by-step guide to inquiry, Trevor MacKenzie and Rebecca Bathurst-Hunt make inquiry-based learning simple.

Sketchnotes for Educators

100 Inspiring Illustrations for Lifelong Learners

By Sylvia Duckworth

Sylvia Duckworth is a Canadian teacher whose sketchnotes have taken social media by storm. Her drawings provide clarity and provoke dialogue on many topics related to education. This book contains 100 of her most popular sketchnotes with links to the original downloads that can be used in class or shared with colleagues. Interspersed throughout the book are Sylvia's reflections on each drawing and what motivated her to create them, in addition to commentary from other educators who inspired the sketchnotes.

How to Sketchnote

A Step-by-Step Manual for Teachers and Students

By Sylvia Duckworth

Educator and internationally known sketchnoter Sylvia Duckworth makes ideas memorable and shareable with her simple yet powerful drawings. In *How to Sketchnote*, she explains how you can use sketchnoting in the classroom and that you don't have to be an artist to discover the benefits of doodling!

40 Ways to Inject Creativity into Your Classroom with Adobe Spark
By Ben Forta and Monica Burns

Experienced educators Ben Forta and Monica Burns offer step-by-step guidance on how to incorporate this powerful tool into your classroom in ways that are meaningful and relevant. They present 40 fun and practical lesson plans suitable for a variety of ages and subjects as well as 15 graphic organizers to get you started. With the tips, suggestions, and encouragement in this book, you'll find everything you need to inject creativity into your classroom using Adobe Spark.

The HyperDoc Handbook
Digital Lesson Design Using Google Apps

By Lisa Highfill, Kelly Hilton, and Sarah Landis

The HyperDoc Handbook is a practical reference guide for all K–12 educators who want to transform their teaching into blended-learning environments. *The HyperDoc Handbook* is a bestselling book that strikes the perfect balance between pedagogy and how-to tips while also providing ready-to-use lesson plans to get you started with HyperDocs right away.

The InterACTIVE Class
Using Technology to Make Learning More Relevant and Engaging in the Elementary Classroom

By Joe and Kristin Merrill

In this practical and idea-packed book, coauthors, classroom teachers, and edtech experts Joe and Kristin Merrill share their personal framework for creating an interACTIVE classroom. You'll find new ways to inspire young learners to grow and to develop grit as they stretch their thinking and abilities.

ABOUT THE AUTHOR

Holly Clark is an education thought-leader, international speaker, best-selling author, and an advocate for students. She is a twenty-plus year educator who has spent over fifteen years teaching in a 1:1 classroom and over five years as an administrator in both public and private schools. She holds a master's degree in instructional design and educational technology from Columbia University in New York City. Her passion is for helping teachers create classrooms where students want to learn and can become the agents of their own thinking and understanding.

She is a National Board Certified Teacher, Google Certified Innovator, and is now the Chief Learning Officer at The Infused Classroom, Inc. She still spends time co-teaching in classrooms where she helps teachers and schools begin the process of putting students at the center of the learning. Holly consults with schools globally on blended learning environments where meaningful pedagogy is infused with the strategic use of technology. She authors a popular education blog, hollyclark.org, and delivers keynotes to audiences worldwide.

Connect with Holly

Blog: hollyclark.org

Instagram and Twitter @HollyClarkEdu

Email: holly@hollyclark.org

Made in United States
North Haven, CT
18 October 2022

25618863R00109